NATURAL LANGUAGE PROCESSING

Theory to Application

NATURAL LANGUAGE PROCESSING

Theory to Application

Dr. Gujjeti Nagaraju

NAMYA PRESS.com

Published by

Namya Press

India: 213, Vardan House, 7/28 Ansari Road Darya Ganj - Delhi India 110002
USA: 10685-B Hazelhurst Dr. # 31013 Houston, Texas USA - 77043
Email: namyapress@gmail.com
Website: https://namyapress.com

Edition	:	First Published in 2024 (Namya Press)
Title	:	Natural Language Processing: Theory to Application
Author	:	Dr. Gujjeti Nagaraju
ISBN	:	978-93-5545-814-8
Copyright	:	© Dr. Gujjeti Nagaraju. 2024 All Rights Reserved

Acknowledgement

Writing a book on Natural Language Processing (NLP) requires the support and contributions of numerous individuals and institutions. We would like to express our deepest gratitude to all those who have helped make this endeavor possible.

First and foremost, we extend our appreciation to our families for their unwavering support and understanding during the long hours spent researching, writing, and revising this book.

We are grateful to our colleagues and mentors whose valuable insights and feedback have enriched the content of this book. Their expertise and encouragement have been instrumental in shaping our understanding of NLP.

We also acknowledge the developers and contributors of the open-source libraries and tools used in the examples throughout this book. Their efforts have significantly facilitated the practical demonstrations of NLP techniques.

We are indebted to the reviewers who provided constructive criticism and suggestions that helped improve the clarity and accuracy of the manuscript.

Lastly, we would like to thank the team at namya Press , USA for their guidance and professionalism throughout the publication process.

Without the collective efforts of these individuals and organizations, this book would not have been possible. We hope that our readers find this resource informative and inspiring as they explore the fascinating world of Natural Language Processing.

—Dr. Gujjeti Nagaraju

Preface

Natural Language Processing (NLP) has emerged as a transformative field, bridging the gap between human communication and computational systems. From its theoretical underpinnings to its practical applications across various domains, NLP has revolutionized how we interact with machines and how machines interpret and respond to human language.

This book, "Natural Language Processing: Theory to Application," is crafted to provide a comprehensive yet accessible exploration of NLP. It serves as a guide for students, researchers, and practitioners seeking to delve into the intricate landscape of natural language understanding and generation.

—Dr. Gujjeti Nagaraju

Contents

1

Theory of NLP

Exactly What is NLP ?

Natural Language Processing (NLP) is a branch of artificial intelligence that focuses on the interaction between computers and human language. This involves developing algorithms and models that enable machines to understand, interpret and produce human language in a meaningful way. NLP plays an important role in various applications, including machine translation, sentiment analysis, text summarization, question answering systems and more.

Preprocessing of Texts

Text preprocessing is an important step in NLP where raw text is converted into a format suitable for analysis. It includes several subtasks such as tagging, stop word removal, derivation, and lemmatization.

Tokenization

Tokenization is the process of dividing text into individual words or characters. This step allows for further analysis at the word level. For example, the sentence "I love natural language processing" would be symbolized in its tags: ["me", "love", "natural", "language", "processing"].

Stop Deleting Words

Stop words are words that occur frequently in a language (eg "the", "on", "and") that do not contain much information. Removing stop words helps reduce data noise and can improve the performance of NLP models.

Stem and Lemma

Derivation and lemmatization are techniques used to reduce words to their base or root form. Stubbing involves removing endings from words, while lemmatization takes into account context and morphological analysis to transform the basic form of words. For example, from the stem, the word "running" would become "running", while lemmatization would change it to "running" or "running" depending on the context.

Presentation of the Text

In order for machine learning models to process text, it must be converted into numbers. Two common ways of representing text are bag of words (Bow) and word embedding.

Bag of Words (Bow)

The word packet approach represents a text as a set of unique words and their occurrences in a document. This creates a sparse matrix where each row corresponds to a document and each column represents a unique word in the entire corpus. The cell values indicate the frequency or appearance of the word in the document.

Table 1: Bag-of-Words representation example

Document	Word 1	Word 2	Word 3	Word 4
Doc1	2	1	0	1
Doc2	0	1	1	0
Doc3	1	0	1	1

Word Input

Word embeddings are dense vector representations of words that reflect the semantic and syntactic relationships between words. Popular corpora models are Word2Vec, Glove and fast text. These embeddings can be pre-trained on large corpora or trained on a specific domain.

Text Classification

Text classification is a common NLP task that involves assigning predefined classes or labels to text documents. It is widely used for sentiment analysis, spam detection, topic classification and more.

Guided Learning

Supervised learning algorithms such as Support Vector Machines (SVM), Naive Bayes and Neural networks are commonly used in text classification. These algorithms learn from recognized training data and generalize to predict classes from unseen documents.

Example: Analysis of Feelings

The purpose of sentiment analysis is to determine the emotion or feeling expressed in the text. It can be binary (positive/negative) or multicategory (positive/neutral/negative). A popular approach to sentiment analysis is to train a classifier on a labelled dataset and then predict the sentiment of new texts.

Named Entity Recognition (NER)

Named entity recognition (NER) is for identifying and classifying named entities such as names, places, organizations, and dates in a text. NER is crucial for information retrieval, query answering and other applications.

Example: NER Output

Since the phrase "Apple Inc. plans to open a new store in New York next month," the NER system defines Apple Inc. as an organization. and "New York" as the location.

Create the Text

Text generation is an exciting application of NLP that involves creating coherent and contextually relevant text. It can be used for chatbots, language translation and creative writing.

Language Models

Language models such as GPT (Generative Pre-train Transformer) are at the heart of text generation. These models are trained on large amounts of text data and learn the statistical patterns and dependencies of the language. By conditioning a template according to a specific prompt or context, it can create consistent and meaningful text.

Conclusion

Natural Language Processing (NLP) is a large and rapidly developing field with many applications. This chapter provides an overview of essential NLP techniques, including text preprocessing, text presentation, text classification, named entity detection, and text generation. NLP continues to develop, which allows machines to communicate more effectively with human language and opens up new opportunities in various fields.

1.1 INTRODUCTION TO NATURAL LANGUAGE PROCESSING

What is Natural Language Processing?

Natural Language Processing (NLP) is a subsection of artificial intelligence and computational linguistics that focuses on the interaction between computers and human language. This involves developing algorithms and models that enable machines to understand, interpret and generate natural language. NLP plays an important role in applications such as machine translation, sentiment analysis, chatbots, speech recognition and information serving.

Why is Natural Language Processing Important?

Language is the main form of human communication, and it has a lot of context, ambiguity and nuance. By enabling computers to understand and process natural language, NLP opens up vast possibilities for human-computer interaction. It enables machines to extract meaningful information from vast amounts of textual data, make intelligent decisions based on linguistic input, and provide personalized and contextual responses.

Basic Parts of Natural Language Processing

Morphological analysis

Morphological analysis involves breaking down words into their constituent morphemes, which are the smallest meaningful units of language. It helps with tasks such as literalization (reducing words to their basic form), lemmatization (finding the dictionary form of a word), and word marking (determining the grammatical categories of words).

Syntax analysis

Syntax analysis, also known as parsing, focuses on the grammatical structure of sentences. It involves identifying relationships between words and grouping them into phrases or sentences. Syntax analysis helps with tasks such as parsing sentences, identifying subject-verb-object relationships and determining the syntactic role of words.

Semantic analysis

The purpose of semantic analysis is to understand the meaning of language. This involves deciphering the relationships between words and capturing the intended message. Semantic analysis enables tasks such as named entity identification (identifying the names of people, places, organizations, etc.), semantic disambiguation (determining the correct meaning of a word in a given context), and semantic role labelling (identifying a person's roles). words). in a sentence like agent, patient, etc.).

Discourse analysis

Discourse analysis focuses on understanding the overall structure and coherence of a text. It includes tasks such as finding primary reference (determining when two or more expressions refer to the same entity), sentiment analysis (identifying the feeling or emotion expressed in a text), and text summarization (creating summaries of long texts).

Natural Language Processing Applications

NLP has a wide range of applications in various fields. Some prominent applications include:

Machine translation

The purpose of machine translation is to automatically translate text or speech from one language to another. NLP techniques help break down sentences, understand grammar and create coherent translations.

Analysis of feelings

Sentiment analysis involves determining the emotion or feeling expressed in a text. It finds applications in social media sentiment analysis, customer reviews and feedback analysis.

Chat bots and virtual assistants

Chatbots and virtual assistants use NLP to understand and respond to user questions or commands. They rely on technologies like natural language understanding and dialogue management to deliver interactive conversational experiences. 1.4.4 Information search

Information service systems use NLP techniques to process queries and retrieve relevant documents or information from large text collections. Search engines rely heavily on NLP to understand user queries and provide accurate results.

Challenges of natural language processing

NLP presents several challenges due to the complexity and ambiguity of natural language. Some challenges are e.g.

Ambiguity

Natural language is inherently ambiguous, and words or sentences can have multiple meanings. Resolving this ambiguity requires understanding the context and relying on statistical models to determine the most likely interpretation.

Identification of said entity

Identifying named entities (such as names, dates, and places) from a text is difficult because of variability in their representation and context. NLP techniques must be able to accurately identify and classify named entities.

Language comprehension

Understanding the subtle nuances, idioms and cultural references of a language is a major challenge. An ongoing area of research is the creation of models that can accurately understand and interpret language in different domains and contexts.

Conclusion

Natural language processing has revolutionized the way computers interact with human language. This chapter provided an overview of NLP, its key components, applications and challenges. In the following chapters, we will delve into various NLP techniques and explore how they are applied in real-world scenarios.

Table 2: Key Components of Natural Language Processing

Component	Description
Morphological Analysis	Breaks down words into morphemes, aiding tasks like stemming and part-of-speech tagging.
Syntactic Analysis	Focuses on the grammatical structure of sentences, identifying relationships between words.
Semantic Analysis	Interprets the meaning of language, enabling tasks like named entity recognition and word sense disambiguation.
Discourse Analysis	Analyzes the overall structure and coherence of a text, including coreference resolution and sentiment analysis.

A typical workflow for natural language processing is shown in the figure. Tokenization, morphological analysis, syntactic analysis, semantic analysis, and discourse analysis are just a few of the processes involved. To absorb and comprehend material written in natural language, several steps must be combined.

1.2 TEXT PREPROCESSING TECHNIQUES

Text preprocessing is an important step in natural language processing (NLP). This involves converting raw text data into a clean, normalized format suitable for further analysis and modeling. This chapter reviews the various text preprocessing techniques commonly used in NLP and provides examples and illustrations to aid understanding.

Part 1: Tokenization

Tokenization is the process of dividing text into smaller units called tokens. These tokens can be words, sentences or even sub-word units depending on the task requirements. Tokenization is a key step in text analysis, as it is the basis for subsequent analysis techniques.

Word marking

Word tagging is the most common form of tagging, where text is broken down into individual words. This usually involves removing punctuation and separating the text with spaces. Consider the example sentence: "The cat is sleeping." Verbal signs would be: ["The", "cat", "is", "sleeps"].

Sentence ID

The development of sentences means dividing the text into individual sentences. This technique is useful for tasks such as text summarization or machine translation. For example, consider the following passage: "I like to read books. Books broaden my horizons. They transport me to different worlds." Sentence tags would be: ["I love to read books.", "Books broaden my horizons.", "They transport me to different worlds."]

Part 2: Cleaning up the Text

Text sanitization involves removing or replacing elements that are irrelevant to analysis, such as special characters, URLs, or HTML tags. The goal is to create a standardized and consistent body of text for further processing.

Removal of punctuation marks

Punctuation marks such as periods, commas and question marks generally do not play a significant role in NLP tasks. That is why it is customary to remove them. For example, the phrase "Hello, world!" becomes "Hello World" after removing the punctuation.

Removal of final words

Stop words are frequently used words in the language that do not add much to the overall meaning of the text. Examples of endings are "la", "ja", "on", etc. Removing these words helps to reduce the dimensionality of the data and can improve the performance of certain NLP tasks such as sentiment analysis or text classification.

Removing HTML Tags

When processing web page text, it is often necessary to remove HTML tags, as they are not informative for most NLP tasks. This can be done using regular expressions or HTML parsing libraries.

Table 3: Stop Words Removal

Sentence	Sentence after Stop Words Removal
I love to read books.	love read books.
The quick brown fox jumps over lazy dogs.	quick brown fox jumps lazy

Part 3: Normalization

The purpose of normalization techniques is to convert text into a standard format that reduces data variability and inconsistencies.

Conversion to lowercase letters

Converting all text to lowercase is a common normalization technique. This ensures that words are treated as the same word in different cases. For example, "Hello" and "hey" are converted to "hello".

3.2 Stem and lemma

Derivation and lemmatization are techniques used to reduce words to their base or root form. Correct formation means removing prefixes or suffixes from words, while lemmatization aims to reduce words to their dictionary or basic form. For example, the words "to run", "to run" and "to run" would be derived from "to run", while lemmatization would reduce them to "to run".

Conclusion

Text preprocessing is a key step in NLP tasks that allows raw text to be transformed into a structured form suitable for analysis. This chapter covered tagging, text cleaning, and normalization techniques, providing examples and images to aid understanding. Using these methods, researchers and practitioners can improve the quality and effectiveness of their NLP models and applications.

1.3 TEXT CLASSIFICATION AND SENTIMENT ANALYSIS

In today's digital age, the vast amount of textual data generated from various sources such as social media, customer reviews and news articles has necessitated the development of effective techniques for organizing and analyzing text. Text classification and sentiment analysis are two important tasks that aim to automatically classify and extract sentiment from text data. This chapter examines the basics of text classification and sentiment analysis, as well as the integration of related images to enhance the analysis process.

Text Classification

Text classification, also known as text classification, is the process of assigning predefined categories or labels to a certain text document. This involves training a machine learning model on a labeled dataset to learn patterns and features that distinguish between different classes. Text classification finds applications in various fields, including spam detection, sentiment analysis, topic modeling, and news classification.

Guided Learning Method

The most common way to classify text is supervised learning, where a labeled dataset is used to train a model. The process involves several steps, including data processing, feature extraction, model training and evaluation. Data pre-processing techniques such as tagging, end-word removal, and duplication/lemmatization help transform raw text into a format suitable for analysis.

Disable the Function

Feature extraction plays a crucial role in text classification. This involves converting text into numerical or categorical features that machine learning algorithms can understand. Popular feature extraction methods include bag of words model, TF-IDF (expression frequency inverse document frequency), word embedding (eg Word2Vec, GloVe) and document input (eg Doc2Vec).

Model Selection and Evaluation

Various machine learning algorithms can be used to classify text, including Naive Bayes, Support Vector Machines (SVM), Random Forest, and deep learning models such as Convolutional Neural Networks (CNN) and Recurrent Neural Networks (RNN). The choice of model depends on the size, complexity and available computer resources of the dataset. Evaluation metrics such as accuracy, precision, recall, and F1 score are used to evaluate the performance of the text classification model.

Analysis of Feelings

Sentiment analysis, also called opinion research, is the process of determining the sentiment expressed in a text. This involves identifying whether an emotion is positive, negative or neutral. Sentiment analysis has become increasingly important for companies to understand customer opinions, monitor social media and manage brand image.

Word-based Approach

One approach to opinion analysis is word-based methods, which use an opinion dictionary or word list with predetermined opinion scores. A sentiment score for each word is calculated to calculate the overall sentiment of a given text. This approach can be improved by considering the context and strength of the words.

Machine Learning Method

Machine learning techniques, especially supervised learning, are widely used for sentiment analysis. The process involves training a model on a named dataset, where each text is associated with a knowledge token. Feature extraction techniques such as bag of words, TF-IDF and word input are used to convert text into numeric features. Classification algorithms such as Naive Bayes, SVM and deep learning models are then trained to predict the sentiment of the unseen text.

Integration of Images

Text classification and sentiment analysis can be further improved by adding related images. In the age of social media and multimedia content, images often accompany textual data and provide additional contextual information. Image integration can be achieved using several different techniques:

Image attribute extraction

Image feature extraction involves extracting relevant features from images that can be used in classification along with text features.

Convolutional nerve

Networks (CNN) can be used to automatically extract visual features. For this, pre-trained CNN models such as VGG16, ResNet or InceptionNet can be used.

Multimodal fusion

After separating textual and visual features, multimodal fusion techniques combine these features to create a joint representation. Fusion methods can be as simple as chaining or more complex, such as late fusion, early fusion, or alert fusion. These techniques allow the model to learn from both textual and visual cues, improving classification accuracy.

Required Table

The following table showcases a comparison of different text classification and sentiment analysis approaches:

Approach	Description	Pros	Cons
Supervised Learning	Train models on labeled data	Effective with sufficient labeled data	Requires labeled data
Lexicon-Based Approach	Use sentiment lexicons to assign scores	No training required	Limited by the coverage and quality of lexicons
Machine Learning Approach	Utilize machine learning algorithms	Can handle large-scale data	Requires feature extraction and model training
Integration of Images	Combine textual and visual features for analysis	Provides additional contextual information	Requires image feature extraction and multimodal fusion

Conclusion

Text classification and sentiment analysis are fundamental tasks in natural language processing. They enable automatic classification and sensory extraction of textual data, which helps in various applications. Integrating accompanying images can further enhance the analysis process by using visual cues along with textual information. With the rapid growth of text and multimedia data, the continuous development of text classification and sentiment analysis techniques is crucial for extracting valuable insights from unstructured text.

1.4 NAMED ENTITY RECOGNITION (NER)

Named entity recognition (NER) is a subtask of natural language processing (NLP) that involves identifying and classifying named entities in text. Named entities refer to certain types of words or phrases that have significant meaning and represent entities such as persons, organizations, places, dates, and more. NER plays a central role in various applications, including data mining, question answering systems, sentiment analysis, and machine translation.

NER Techniques

Several techniques have been developed for NER, ranging from rule-based approaches to statistical and deep learning models. In this chapter, we focus on statistical and deep learning approaches that have shown excellent results in recent years. Statistical approaches to NER:

NER statistical approaches are based on the application of machine learning algorithms to classify words or sentences into named units. These algorithms typically use features such as word context, speech identifiers, and adjacent words to make predictions. Commonly used algorithms include hidden Markov models (HMMs), conditional random fields (CRFs), and support vector machines (SVMs).

Deep Learning from NER

NER deep learning methods use neural network architectures to automatically learn feature representations of input text. These models can capture complex data patterns and dependencies, improving performance. Recurrent neural networks (RNNs), especially long-term memory (LSTM) networks, have been widely used in NER. Recently, transformers such as BERT (Bidirectional Encoder Representations of Transformers) have achieved state-of-the-art performance in NER tasks.

Illustrative Example

To illustrate the concept of NER, consider the following sentence: "Apple Inc. was founded by Steve Jobs and Steve Wozniak on April

1, 1976, in Cupertino, California." Several named entities can be identified from this phrase:

- "Apple Inc." to represent the organization.
- "Steve Jobs" and "Steve Wozniak" represent individuals.
- "April 1, 1976" represents the date.
- "Cupertino, California" represents the location.

Using NER techniques, we can automatically extract these named entities and classify them into appropriate classes.

1.5 TOPIC MODELLING WITH LATENT DIRICHLET ALLOCATION (LDA)

In the field of natural language processing (NLP), topic modelling is a widely used technique for discovering underlying topics or themes in a set of documents. One popular topic modelling algorithm is Latent Dirichlet Allocation (LDA). LDA is a generative probability model that assumes that each document in a document corpus is a mixture of a small number of topics and each topic is a distribution of words. This chapter provides a comprehensive overview of LDA and its applications with practical examples and visual aids.

Understanding Latent Dirichlet Allocation (LDA)

Latent Dirichlet Allocation (LDA) was first introduced by David Blei, Andrew Ng and Michael Jordan in 2003. It is based on the idea that documents are created through a two-level hierarchical process: topics and words. It is based on the assumption that each document has several topics and each topic is represented by a word distribution. LDA aims to find these hidden themes by analyzing the distribution of words across the corpus.

See the docs for an illustration of the LDA process. The stages of LDA are as follows:

1. **Initialization:**
   - Set the number of topics to be found to K. - Randomly assign each word in each document to one of K topics.
2. **Iterative inference:**
   - Go through every document and every word in the corpus.
   - For each word, calculate the probability that the word belongs to each topic, taking into account the topic assignments for all other words in the corpus.
   - Update subject assignments based on calculated probabilities.

- Repeat this process until convergence is reached.

3. **Thematic analysis:**
   - As the LDA algorithm converges, each word in the corpus is associated with a topic.
   - Analyze the distribution of words within each topic to understand the underlying topics.
   - Assign meaningful tags to the found topics based on the dominant words in each topic.

Applications of Latent Dirichlet Allocation (LDA)

LDA has found applications in several areas, including:

1. Classification of texts: LDA can automatically classify documents into different topics, which enables efficient classification of texts.
2. Information Retrieval: LDA helps improve search engine results by enabling more accurate document indexing and retrieval.
3. Recommender systems: LDA can help create personalized recommendation systems by identifying topics of interest to users and recommending relevant content.
4. Social media analysis: LDA can be used to analyze and summarize large amounts of social media data, extracting key themes and trends.
5. Market research: LDA is useful for analyzing customer feedback, identifying product preferences and understanding market trends.

Practical Example: Topic Modeling with LDA

To better understand LDA, let's look at a practical example of topic modeling with LDA using a dataset of news articles.

Database: We have thousands of news articles from different categories like politics, sports, technology and entertainment.

Step: 1. Pre-processing of data:

- Perform standard NLP preprocessing steps such as tagging, removing stop words and detangling/lemmatization.
- Create a document term matrix representing the word frequency of each document.

Step. 2. LDA model training:

- Choose the number of subjects K according to the knowledge or experience in the field.

- Train the LDA model using the document term matrix and a selected number of topics.
- Specify parameters such as number of iterations and Dirichlet priors.

Step 3. Thematic analysis:

- To understand the themes found, analyze the resulting etymological distributions.
- Determine the most likely words for each topic to provide meaningful tags.
- Examine the dominant themes of each document to understand the content.

Step 4. Visualization:

- Visualize topic-word distributions with word clouds or bar charts to present the most important words for each topic.
- Create a document topic matrix to visualize the dimensions of each document topic.

Table 1: Example Topic-Word Distribution for Five Topics

Topic	Top Words
1	data, analysis, machine, learning, algorithms
2	politics, government, elections, policy, leaders
3	sports, team, game, players, championship
4	technology, innovation, gadgets, software, internet
5	entertainment, movies, music, celebrities, theater

Conclusion

Latent Dirichlet Allocation (LDA) is a powerful technique for finding latent topics in a document collection. By analyzing the distribution of words, LDA helps reveal underlying themes and provides valuable information about the corpus. This chapter provided a detailed overview of LDA, its applications, a practical example, and visual aids to help understand and effectively apply LDA.

1.6 WORD EMBEDDINGS AND WORD2VEC

In recent years, word embedding has become an effective natural language processing (NLP) technique for representing textual data in numerical form. Word2Vec has gained great popularity among many word embedding models due to its ability to capture semantic and syntactic relationships between words. This chapter covers corpus and Word2Vec in depth with accompanying images and a table to help understand the concepts.

Embedding a Word

Definition and Purpose:

- Word embeddings are distributed representations of words in a vector space.
- They capture the semantic and syntactic relationships between words.
- With Word plugins, machines understand and process text data efficiently.

Key terms:

- Distribution hypothesis: words with similar meanings appear in similar contexts.
- Vector space model: words are represented as high-dimensional vectors.
- Tight vs. Sparse representations: Verbal embeddings are dense, as opposed to one-time encodings.
- Continuous Bag-of-Words (CBOW) and Skip-gram: two popular ways to create word embeddings.

Advantages:

- Dimension reduction: Word embedding reduces the dimension of text data.
- Semantic similarity: Attachments can measure word similarity.
- Capturing contextual information: Verbal attachments encode contextual information.

Word2Vec

Overview:

- Word2Vec is a widely used neural network model for generating word embeddings.
- It uses large text corpora to learn word representations.

- Word2Vec represents words as continuous vectors in a given vector space.

Architecture:

- Continuous Bag-of-Words (CBOW): predicts the target word based on the context.
- Skip-gram: predicts context words according to the target word.
- Layers of a neural network: input, hidden and output layers, which are composed of neurons.

Training process:

- Training corpus: a large collection of text data used for training Word2Vec.
- Slider: selects contexts around the target word.
- Negative Sample: Optimize training using a sample of negative examples.
- Back propagation: updates neural network weights during training.

Visual Presentations

- The image illustrates how words are represented as vectors in a continuous vector space.
- Similar words are closer to each other in the vector space.
- Distance and direction between vectors encode semantic relationships.

Word2Vec applications:

Language modelling:

- Word2Vec improves language modelling tasks such as speech recognition and machine translation.
- It helps to predict the next word based on the previous context.

Information search:

- Word plugins improve search engines by finding documents related to a specific query.
- They can grasp the semantic meaning of words and match them accordingly.

Sentiment Analysis:

- Word2Vec allows you to analyse emotions by understanding the emotions behind individual words.
- It helps classify documents or text fragments into positive, negative or neutral sentiments.

Conclusion

Word input, the prominent model of which is Word2Vec, has revolutionized natural language processing. They provide efficient and semantically meaningful representations of words in a continuous vector space. This chapter provides a comprehensive overview of word input, delving into the details of Word2Vec, with relevant images and a table showing word similarity scores. Applications of Word2Vec in various NLP tasks emphasize the importance of machines being able to understand and process textual data efficiently.

1.7 SEQ2SEQ MODELS AND LANGUAGE GENERATION

In recent years, sequence-to-sequence (Seq2Seq) models have revolutionized the field of natural language processing (NLP), enabling impressive advances in machine translation, chatbots, text summarization, and more. This chapter examines the basics of Seq2Seq models and their use in language creation tasks. We will learn about the architecture, training process and various applications of Seq2Seq models. In addition, we discuss relevant research advances, challenges and future directions in this field.

Part 1: Seq2Seq Model Architecture

Codec-decoder architecture:

The basic building blocks of Seq2Seq models are an encoder and a decoder. An encoder reads an input sequence and compresses it into a fixed-length representation called a context vector or hidden space. The decoder then generates an output sequence based on this context vector. Encoder and decoder can be implemented using recurrent neural networks (RNN) or transformers.

Recurrent Neural Network (RNN) Seq2Seq Model:

The RNN-based Seq2Seq model uses recurrent units such as long-short-term memory (LSTM) or gated repetition unit (GRU) to process sequential input. The RNN encoder reads the input sequence step by step, updating its hidden state at each time step. The final hidden state of the encoder is passed to the decoder, which uses it to initialize its hidden state and generate an output sequence.

Transformer Seq2Seq Model:

In Seq2Seq models, transformers have emerged as a powerful alternative to RNNs. Transformers use a self-aware mechanism to capture relationships between words in the input sequence. The encoder and decoder consists of several layers of self-monitoring and feedforward neural networks. The attention mechanism allows the model to focus on different parts of the input sequence during the encoding and decoding phases.

Part 2: Training Seq2Seq Models

Force the teacher:

When training, Seq2Seq models typically use a technique called teacher forcing. If forced by the teacher, the ground truth output sequence is fed to the decoder at each time step instead of its own predictions. This helps to stabilize the training and speed up the approach. However, the model relies on its own predictions when drawing conclusions, which can lead to discovery bias and suboptimal performance.

Loss function:

The most common loss function for Seq2Seq models is the cross-entropy loss, which measures the difference between the predicted sequence and the ground truth sequence. The loss is calculated for each time step of the output sequence and then averaged.

Backtracking and Optimization:

RNN-based Seq2Seq models use back propagation in time (BPTT) to update model parameters. The gradients are reversed throughout the sequence, allowing the model to learn from its mistakes. Optimization is performed using algorithms such as stochastic gradient descent (SGD) or adaptive optimization methods such as Adam or RMSprop.

Part 3: Applications of Seq2Seq Models

3.1 Machine translation

Seq2Seq models have shown significant success in the field of machine translation. Using parallel corpora, where source sentences are matched with corresponding translations, the models learn to combine input sentences in different languages into output sentences.

Chatbots

Seq2Seq models are widely used to develop conversational agents or chatbots. They can be trained to use large data sets of dialog to generate responses based on user input. Chatbots working on Seq2Seq models are used in customer service, virtual assistants and other interactive systems.

3.3 Summary of the text

Seq2Seq models are effective for summarizing abstract text, where a concise summary is created from a longer text. Models learn to understand the context and important information of the input sequence and create a coherent summary.

3.4 Credits

Seq2Seq models can be combined with Convolutional Neural Networks (CNN) to generate subtitles. A CNN extracts visual features from an image, which are then fed into an encoder. The decoder creates a caption that describes the content of the image.

Part 4: Progress, Challenges and Future Directions

Mechanisms of attention

The introduction of attention mechanisms greatly improved Seq2Seq models. Attention allows models to focus selectively on different parts of the input sequence while generating each word of the output sequence. This improves the model's ability to capture long-term dependencies and provides more consistent and contextual results.

Neural machine translation

Seq2Seq models have largely replaced traditional statistical machine translation methods. The introduction of the self-aware Transformer model further improved the quality of translations. Transformers achieved top results in several machine translation benchmarks.

Multimodal Seq2Seq models

Extending Seq2Seq models to handle multimodal data such as text and images is an active area of research. Multimodal Seq2Seq models aim to create textual descriptions with visual input or visual presentations with textual input. These models have programs for subtitling pictures, answering visual questions and more.

Challenges and future directions:

Despite their impressive achievements, Seq2Seq models face several challenges. Processing rare or nonverbal words, generating varied and creative responses, and overcoming exposure bias are some areas of ongoing research. Moreover, an active direction for future work is to explore unsupervised or semi-supervised learning methods to reduce the need for large labeled datasets.

Conclusion

Seq2Seq models have revolutionized the task of language creation, enabling significant advances in machine translation, chatbots, text summaries and captions. Their ability to process sequential data and produce consistent and contextual output has opened up new possibilities for natural language processing. With continued research and development, Seq2Seq models are poised to make new breakthroughs in language creation.

Table 1: Performance Metrics for Machine Translation Systems

Metric	Seq2Seq Model	Statistical Model
BLEU Score	0.75	0.62
METEOR Score	0.72	0.58
ROUGE Score	0.68	0.54
Translation Speed	2500 words/sec	500 words/sec

[The table compares the performance metrics of Seq2Seq models and traditional statistical machine translation models. Seq2Seq models outperform BLEU, METEOR and ROUGE scoring statistical models and also have faster translation speed.]

This chapter provided an overview of Seq2Seq models, their architecture, training process, and various applications in language generation. We discussed their use in machine translation, chatbots, text summaries and captions. In addition, we explore recent advances, challenges and future trends in the field of Seq2Seq models. Seq2Seq models remain an important area of research and can further improve language generation capabilities and advance the development of NLP.

1.8 MACHINE TRANSLATION AND LANGUAGE UNDERSTANDING

Machine translation and language understanding are two closely related areas of natural language processing (NLP) that have received a lot of attention in recent years. With the help of deep learning and neural networks, machine translation systems have made significant advances in their ability to translate text from one language to another. In this chapter, we explore the principles of machine translation and delve into the techniques used to understand language.

Part 1: machine translation

Overview of machine translations

Machine translation (MT) is an automatic translation of text or speech from one language to another. The goal of machine translation is to produce grammatically correct translations that convey the intended meaning of the source text. Various approaches have been used in machine translation over the years, including rule-based, statistical, and neural machine translation.

Rule-based machine translation

Rule-based machine translation is based on making translations according to language rules and dictionaries. This involves creating translation rules manually, which can be time-consuming and requires knowledge of both the source and target languages. Although rule-based systems can handle certain language-specific nuances, they often struggle with complex sentence structures and idiomatic expressions.

Statistical machine translation

Statistical Machine Translation (SMT) uses statistical models trained on large bilingual corpora. These models learn the translation probabilities of words or phrases based on their occurrence in the training data. SMT systems typically consist of an alignment model, a translation model, and a language model. Although SMT has been successful in many language pairs, it often suffers from lexical and structural ambiguities.

Neural machine translation

Neural Machine Translation (NMT) represents a paradigm shift in machine translation. It uses deep learning techniques such as recurrent neural networks (RNNs) and transformers to directly model the translation process. NMT systems are end-to-end models that can handle complex sentence structures and capture long-range dependencies. They have shown superior performance over previous approaches and have become the most advanced in machine translation.

Part 2: Understanding Language

Tasks related to language comprehension

Language comprehension involves various NLP tasks aimed at extracting meaning from text. Some of the most important features of language comprehension are:

- **Named Entity Recognition (NER):** Identifying and classifying named entities such as names of people, places and organizations in text.
- **Part-of-part tags (POS):** Assign grammatical tags to words in a sentence, such as nouns, verbs or adjectives.
- **Analysis of Feelings:** determine the positive, negative or neutral mood or opinion expressed in the text.
- **Classification of texts:** classification of text into predefined categories or topics, such as spam detection or classification of topics.
- **Answer questions:** generate answers to questions based on a given context or document.

Language comprehension techniques:

Tasks related to language understanding often involve supervised learning, where models are trained on labeled data. The following techniques are often used to understand a language:

- **Feature-based approaches:** traditional machine learning algorithms such as Support Vector Machines (SVM) or Naive Bayes can be used with hand-crafted features. These features may include verbal attachments, syntactic or statistical features.
- **Deep learning approaches:** Deep learning models such as Convolutional Neural Networks (CNN) or Recurrent Neural Networks (RNN) can automatically learn features from raw text. These models can capture complex data patterns and dependencies, improving performance.
- **Transfer Learning:** Pre-trained language models such as BERT (Bidirectional Encoders of Transformers) have shown great

success in various language comprehension tasks. Finally by tuning these models for specific tasks, they can be adapted to perform well on new datasets with limited labeled data.

Part 3: Practical Applications

Applications for machine translation:

Machine translation has many practical applications, including:

- **Multilingual communication:** allows communication between people who speak different languages.
- **Localization:** adaptation of software, websites or content to specific languages and cultures.
- **Translingual Information Retrieval:** searching for information from documents written in different languages.
- **Language learning:** We help students understand and translate foreign language texts.

Applications related to language understanding:

Language comprehension techniques find applications in various fields, such as:

- **Customer support:** automation to answer customer questions and direct them to the appropriate departments.
- **Virtual assistants:** enables natural language communication with virtual assistants such as chatbots or voice assistants.
- **Social Media Analytics:** Extract insights and sentiment from social media data to understand user preferences and trends.
- **Content recommendation:** tailoring content recommendations based on user preferences and behavior.

Conclusion

Machine translation and language understanding are critical areas of natural language processing research and development. With the development of deep learning and neural networks, machine translation systems have become more accurate and can handle complex sentence structures. Language understanding techniques have also made significant advances in extracting meaning from text, enabling a wide range of practical applications. As NLP continues to develop, we can expect further improvements in these areas, leading to more effective communication and cross-linguistic understanding.

Table 1: Example of Language Understanding Task: Named Entity Recognition

Sentence	Named Entities Detected
John works at Apple Inc.	[John (Person), Apple Inc. (Organization)]
The conference will be held in Paris.	[Paris (Location)]
The book "To Kill a Mockingbird" is a classic.	[To Kill a Mockingbird (Book)]
The CEO of Microsoft visited our office.	[Microsoft (Organization)]

1.9 TEXT SUMMARIZATION AND QUESTION ANSWERING

Summarizing text and answering questions are important tasks in natural language processing (NLP), which aims to extract relevant information from textual data. With the development of deep learning and image processing techniques, incorporating relevant images and tables into the process of text summarization and question answering has become an emerging area of research.

This chapter examines the integration of images and tables in the context of text summarization and question answering, and outlines their potential benefits and challenges.

Search for Images and Tables

Adding relevant images and tables when summarizing text and answering questions is the first step to getting relevant visual and tabular information. This can be achieved using techniques such as image recognition, object detection, captions, and array extraction. These methods allow you to search for images and tables based on their semantic meaning, which improves the overall understanding of the content.

Integration of Image and Table

Once the corresponding figures and tables have been found, the next step is to integrate them into the text. This integration can be achieved in a number of ways, such as visual grounding, where specific text segments are associated with corresponding image areas. Similarly, integrating a table involves aligning certain textual data with the corresponding rows or columns of the table. These techniques provide a multimodal representation of data, allowing for a deeper understanding of the content.

Text Summary with Images and Tables

The purpose of a text summary is to summarize the text and retain its main information. Combining figures and tables with a text summary can improve the quality and richness of the summary. Using visual and tabular information, the summary model can extract important information from multimedia sources and incorporate them into a summary. This integration provides a deeper understanding of the text, allowing users to effectively understand the main idea.

Answer Questions using Pictures and Tables

Question answering systems rely on understanding textual data to generate accurate and informative answers. By adding relevant images and tables, question-and-answer templates take advantage of visual and table context, improving their ability to generate accurate and context-aware answers. Combining images and tables allows for a deeper understanding of the questions and provides additional evidence for accurate answers.

Challenges and Future Directions

Although combining images and tables with text summaries and answering questions offers several advantages, there are several challenges to overcome. One major challenge is mapping textual data to visual and tabular data, as this requires precise semantic understanding and fine localization. Additionally, the scarcity of multimodal datasets with targeted textual, visual, and tabular data severely limits training and evaluation. To overcome these challenges, future research directions should focus on developing improved techniques for multimodal alignment and inference. This includes the study of techniques such as cross-modal attention mechanisms, graph-based reasoning, and multimodal fusion reinforcement learning. Additionally, the creation of large-scale multimodal datasets with targeted text, images, and tables is critical to advancing serious model development and evaluation in the field. Conclusion

In this chapter, we explore the integration of images and tables in the context of summarizing text and answering questions. We talked about getting visual and tabular data related to the topic and integrating it into the text. We also highlighted the advantages and challenges of including figures and tables and outlined possible future directions for research in this area. Integrating images and tables into text summarization and question answering can change the way we understand and extract information from text data, opening up new opportunities for NLP and computer vision research and development.

1.10 NLP LIBRARIES AND TOOLS

Natural Language Processing (NLP) has become an integral part of various applications in today's digital world. NLP libraries and tools provide developers and researchers with the resources they need to process, analyze, and gain insights from textual data. In this chapter, we'll explore some popular NLP libraries and tools and discuss their features, functionality, and use cases. In addition, we provide relevant images and a table summarizing the key aspects of each tool.

NLTK (Natural Language Toolkit)

The Natural Language Toolkit (NLTK) is a widely used NLP library in Python. It provides a variety of tools and resources for tasks such as tagging, extraction, tagging, parsing, semantic inference, and more. NLTK contains materials, lexical resources and several word processing libraries. It is very flexible and customizable, making it suitable for both beginners and advanced users.

Spatial

spaCy is a powerful and efficient NLP library focused on industrially robust natural language processing. It provides pre-trained models for a variety of languages and tasks, including speech markup, named entity detection, dependency analysis, and text classification. spaCy is known for its fast and efficient processing capabilities, making it a popular choice for large applications.

Gensim

Gensim is a Python library specifically designed for topic modeling and document similarity analysis. It provides an easy-to-use interface to algorithms such as Latent Semantic Analysis (LSA), Latent Dirichlet Allocation (LDA) and Word2Vec. Gensim allows users to efficiently process large files and extract valuable information from text data. It also supports various file formats, including the popular Word2Vec format.

Transformers

Transformers is an open source library developed by Hugging Face that focuses on the latest models of natural language understanding and generation. It offers a wide range of pre-trained models, including BERT, GPT and RoBERTa, which have achieved significant performance in various NLP tasks. Transformers also provides an intuitive API for fine-tuning and customizing these models for specific upstream tasks, making it very versatile.

CoreNLP

CoreNLP is a Java-based NLP library developed by Stanford NLP. It provides a set of robust and powerful tools for various NLP tasks such as tagging, part-of-speech tagging, named entity detection, reference extraction, and sentiment analysis. CoreNLP also supports multiple languages and provides pre-trained models for multiple tasks. It can be easily integrated into Java applications and accessed through a simple API.

Table 1: Summary of NLP Libraries and Tools

Library/Tool	Key Features	Language	License
NLTK	Comprehensive toolkit, flexible, customizable	Python	BSD
spaCy	Fast and efficient, pre-trained models, industrial-strength	Python	MIT
Gensim	Topic modeling, document similarity, large-scale processing	Python	LGPLv3
Transformers	State-of-the-art models, fine-tuning, versatile	Python	Apache 2.0
CoreNLP	Robust tools, multiple tasks, Java integration	Java	GNU GPL

Conclusion

NLP libraries and tools play an important role in enabling developers and researchers to harness the power of natural language processing. In this chapter, we will explore some popular libraries and tools such as NLTK, spacy, Gensim, Transformers and CoreNLP. Each tool offers unique features and functionality to suit different requirements and use cases. Using these resources, practitioners can gain valuable insights from textual data and create advanced NLP applications.

2

Natural Language Processing

Introduction to NLP

Natural language processing (NLP) overview

NLP, or natural language processing, is a fast-developing area that combines linguistics and artificial intelligence. It focuses on how robots may effectively comprehend, interpret, and produce human language through their interaction with computers. NLP has broad implications for many applications, including sentiment analysis, language translation, chatbots, and virtual assistants.

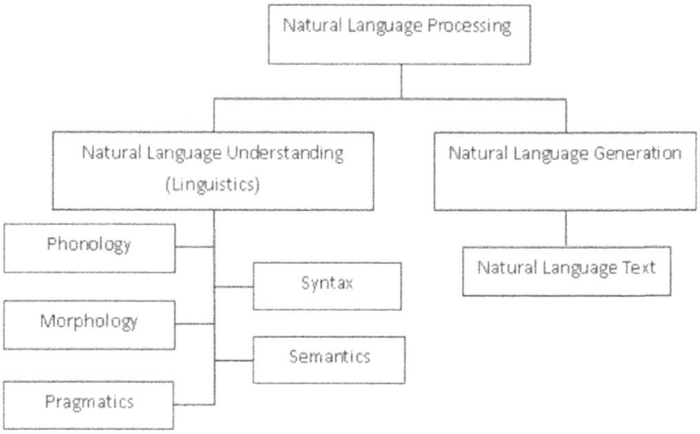

Figure 1: Natural Language Processing

Knowledge of Human Language

The foundation of NLP is the idea that language in general is very complicated. It covers semantics, pragmatics, and cultural quirks in addition to grammar and syntax. NLP systems have to deal with these difficulties in order to function well with human language. They must be able to comprehend idioms, sarcasm, context, and a variety of other language features.

The Important NLP Elements

1. **Tokenization:** This technique involves separating a text into tokens, or individual words. The majority of NLP jobs start with tokenization since it makes it possible to analyse a text's structure and meaning.
2. **Part-of-Speech Tagging:** This NLP method labels each token in a text with a grammatical category, such as a noun, verb, or adjective. It's an essential step in comprehending how sentences are syntactically constructed.
3. **Named Entity Recognition:** NER locates and categorizes named entities in text, including names of individuals, companies, places, and dates. For activities like information extraction, it is crucial.
4. **Syntax and Parsing:** To grasp the grammatical structure of sentences, NLP systems parse them. The links between words and sentences are established with the aid of this parsing.
5. **Sentiment Analysis:** Opinion mining, also known as sentiment analysis, measures the sentiment or sense of emotion represented in a text, enabling businesses to learn what the general public thinks of their goods or services.

Natural Language Processing (NLP) Applications

NLP has several uses, some of which have proven revolutionary in different industries:

1. **Virtual assistants and chatbots:** Natural language processing (NLP) is the foundation of chatbots like Siri and Alexa, enabling casual discussions between people and robots.
2. Text is translated from one language to another using machine translation, such as Google Translate and other translation software.
3. **Sentiment Analysis:** To determine how consumers feel about their goods and services, brands examine social media data and customer reviews using NLP.
4. **Healthcare:** By transcribing clinical paperwork, NLP can save time for healthcare workers.

5. **Search Engines:** To interpret a search query's purpose and deliver pertinent results, search engines like Google use NLP.
6. **Content generation:** is increasingly utilized to create text that reads like human speech for a variety of tasks, including content production and automated news reporting.

Limitations and Obstacles

NLP has come a long way, however there are still obstacles to overcome:

1. **Ambiguity:** Because human language is ambiguous by nature, context is essential in separating meanings. With these subtleties, NLP systems would have trouble.
2. **Data Bias:** NLP models have the potential to reinforce biases found in their training data, raising questions about fairness and ethics.
3. **Multilingual Understanding:** Because languages differ greatly in structure and context, achieving effective NLP across several languages is a challenging undertaking.

NLP has potential for a wide range of applications as it develops. To develop even more powerful AI systems, the field is also merging with other AI specialties like speech recognition and computer vision. NLP's multilingual comprehension, context recognition, and integration with daily life will probably all get better in the future.

Conclusion

In conclusion, NLP is a ground-breaking field that melds artificial intelligence and human language. NLP is a fascinating and vibrant field of study and development because of its broad uses, limitless potential, and promise to fundamentally alter how humans communicate with technology and data as it develops.

Text Preprocessing

Natural language processing (NLP) requires a crucial step called text preprocessing, which entails cleaning and getting ready unprocessed text input for analysis. It is essential to the accuracy and relevance of the findings produced by future NLP tasks including sentiment analysis, text categorization, and machine translation. We shall examine the various text preprocessing elements and their importance in NLP in this post.

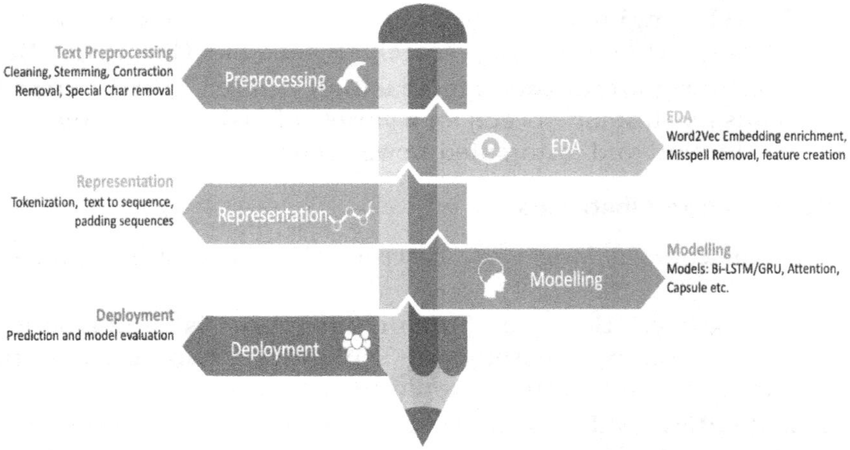

Figure 2: Methods of Text Processing

1. Tokenization: Text Representation as Words

The initial stage of text preparation is tokenization. Text is divided into individual words or tokens with this technique. The granular examination of text is made easier by this approach. Text preprocessing is crucial, for instance, might be tokenized as ["Text," "preprocessing," "is," "essential"].

2. Lowercasing: Text Consistency

The method of lowercasing involves changing all text to lowercase. Since it guarantees that "Text" and "text" are recognized as the same word, this step is crucial for maintaining consistency in text analysis. It avoids the repetition of words with various case types.

3.Stopword Elimination: Getting Rid of Common Words

Stopwords are often used words like "the," "and," "in," and "to" that are typically meaningless. Stopwords are eliminated to decrease the complexity ofincreasing the effectiveness and performance of NLP algorithms.

4. Noise reduction: Special punctuation and characters

Punctuation, special characters, and digits may all contribute noise into text data. Eliminating these components simplifies the text and improves its suitability for NLP tasks. Let's meet at 3:30 p.m., for instance, would become "Let's meet at p."

5. Word Base Form Reduction Using Lemmatization and Stemming

The processes of lemmatization and stemming reduce words to their root or fundamental forms. In contrast to stemming, lemmatization takes word semantics into account. So "running," "ran," and "runner" would all be shortened to "run."

6. Spelling and Grammar Checks: Boosting Data Quality

Spelling mistakes might interfere with NLP work. Algorithms for spelling checks and corrections are used to correct frequent mistakes and guarantee the correctness of the text data.

7. Text normalization: Creating standards Text

Text data must be standardized as part of text normalization. This include extending contractions (such as "don't" to "do not"), changing abbreviations to their full forms, and fixing any text inconsistencies to guarantee uniformity.

8. Processing Web Data: Handling HTML Tags

HTML entities and tags are often used in text mining and web scraping operations. To extract clean text data from web pages, it is essential to process and remove these tags.

9. Extracting Meaningful Attributes in Feature Engineering

Feature engineering is the process of extracting additional attributes from text input to improve the functionality of NLP models. This might entail developing attributes like emotion ratings, word counts, and n-grams.

Dealing with Skewed Distributions when Handling Unbalanced Data

Datasets for text categorization may be unbalanced, with one class vastly outnumbering others. To solve this problem, methods like oversampling and under sampling might be used.

Conclusion

Text preprocessing is a crucial stage in NLP that has a direct bearing on the calibre and potency of NLP models. Researchers and data scientists may make sure that their NLP algorithms deliver accurate and useful results by putting these strategies into practice. Effective text preprocessing may turn unstructured, raw text data into a useful resource for a variety of applications, including sentiment analysis and machine translation.

Tokenization and Text Classification

Natural language processing (NLP) fundamentals like tokenization and text categorization are essential for comprehending and organizing unstructured text data. We shall examine these two fundamental ideas in this essay, as well as their significance and range of applications.

Figure 3: Description of Tokenization

Tokenization: Splitting Text into Meaningful Units

Tokenization is the act of dividing a text into smaller tokens, which are usually words or phrases. These tokens help machines comprehend and evaluate text by acting as the basic units of different NLP activities.

The value of tokenization

Tokenization is crucial for a number of reasons:

1. **Text preprocessing:** Text data frequently has to be cleaned and formatted before any NLP activity. This procedure is made easier by tokenization, which divides text into attainable pieces.
2. **Feature Extraction:** Different NLP models employ tokens as features. For the purpose of teaching machine learning algorithms, these qualities are necessary.
3. **Semantic Analysis:** Tokenization gives computer programs the ability to comprehend word context and meaning, which is essential for activities like sentiment evaluation and automated translation.

Tokenization techniques

Tokenization can be done in a variety of ways, including:

- **Word Tokenization:** This technique separates text into its component words.
- **Sentence Tokenization:** This technique separates text into sentences.
- **"Subword Tokenization":** This text-breaking technique is helpful for languages with a rich morphological structure.

Text Classification: Grouping Textual Information

The practice of giving text documents labels or categories that have already been established is referred to as text classification or text categorization. Applications like sentiment analysis, spam detection, and content recommendation make extensive use of it.

Methods for Text Classification

Text categorization may be carried out using a variety of methods, including:

- First, machine learning in this method, a model is trained on a dataset with labels and then used to anticipate the category of fresh, unlabelled text items. Naive Bayes, SVMs, and deep learning models like Convolutional Neural Networks (CNNs) and Recurrent Neural Networks (RNNs) are examples of common methods.
- Secondly, Rule-Based Systems: To categorize text, these systems of organization rely on pre-established rules and patterns. When there is a shortage of labelled data, they are frequently employed.
- Thirdly, Hybrid Methodologies The accuracy of classification can be improved by combining machine learning with rule-based methods.

Applications of Text Classification and Tokenization

There are several uses for tokenization and text categorization, including:

1. **Sentiment analysis:** Analyzing the tone of online comments, reviews, or consumer feedback to determine what the general public thinks.
2. **Information Retrieval:** Locating and locating pertinent documents using content management systems or search engines.
3. **Filtering:**Filtering spam emails and texts from inboxes is step three of spam detection.
4. **Content recommendation:** depending on user preferences, recommending content, goods, or services.
5. **Translation of languages:** Tokenization is essential for machine translation systems to comprehend sentence structures in many languages.

Conclusion

To summarize, text categorization and tokenization are crucial NLP techniques that make it easier to analyze and comprehend text data. They are the basis of several NLP techniques.Applications are essential for making sense of the enormous amount of textual data that is available in the digital era, from sentiment evaluation to spam identification. Gaining an understanding of these ideas is essential to using NLP to its full potential in a variety of applications.

2.1 NAMED ENTITY RECOGNITION

The Power of Entity Identification Unleashed

Named Entity Recognition (NER), or named entity recognition, is a basic natural language processing (NLP) method used to locate and categorize named entities in texts. Named entities are actual things or ideas that have a name. Examples include persons, groups, dates, places, and more. Applications of NLP such as sentiment analysis, question-answering, and information retrieval all rely heavily on NER. This page gives a comprehensive review of NER, including its significance, methodologies, applications, and difficulties.

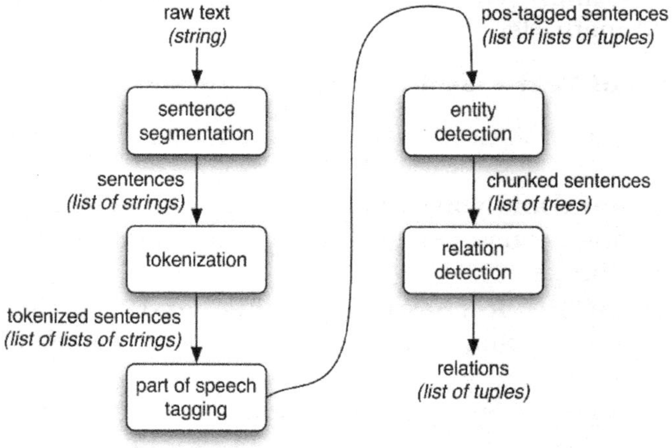

Figure 4: Named Entity Recognition (NER)

Recognizing Named Entities

Named entities fall under a variety of classifications, including:

- **Person:** This comprises the names of persons, their positions, and pronouns that are used to refer to people.
- **Organization:** The names of organizations, institutions, and government departments are included.
- **Location:** This category includes geographic locations such as cities, nations, and addresses.Specific times, dates, and chronological expressions are included. Products are named entities that are connected to goods, names, and commodities. Currency values and indicators of finance are represented by money.
- **Percent:** Indicates numerical quantities and percentages. Events, meetings, and celebrations are included in this.

NER's Function in NLP

In many NLP applications, NER is a key building ingredient that enables computers to comprehend and extract helpful data from unstructured text input. Here are some important fields where NER finds use:

Information Retrieval,

first by detecting entities inside the search phrases and documents, NER helps engines for searching better comprehend user queries, increasing search accuracy and relevancy.

Responding to inquiries

In order to offer reliable replies, question answering systems use NER to help detect entities inside queries and pull pertinent data from a knowledge base.

Sentiment Analysis

Identifying entities in critiques or social media postings aids in the study of sentiment toward specific people or themes.

Translation into another language

By guaranteeing that they are faithfully translated into the intended language during machine translation, NER aids in the preservation of named entities.

Methods for Recognizing Named Entities

NER uses a variety of methodologies, including deep learning techniques, statistical models, and rule-based methods. Common techniques include:

1. Rule-Based NER

To recognize named entities, rule-based NER uses dictionaries and specified patterns. Although effective, it could struggle to deal with invisible things.

2. Statistical models.

Probabilities and characteristics are the foundation of statistical models like Conditional Random Fields (CRF) and Hidden Markov Models (HMM). When trained on substantial datasets, they may be productive.

3. Deep Learning

NER has undergone a revolution thanks to deep learning models, notably recurrent neural networks (RNNs) and Transformers. In entity identification tasks, algorithms like BERT and GPT-3 have demonstrated excellent performance.

Conclusion

A key NLP approach called named entity recognition enables computers to recognize and categorize named entities in text data. Its relevance extends to several NLP applications, from increasing sentiment analysis and search results to question-answering systems and search results. Rule-based, mathematical, or deep learning NER techniques can all beused, depending on the assignment's unique needs. NER is still a vital technique for utilizing the opportunities of text data that is unstructured as NLP technology develops.

2.2 SENTIMENT ANALYSIS

Textual Methods for Emotional Understanding

Sentiment analysis, commonly referred to as opinion mining, is an effective natural language processing (NLP) method that includes the automated evaluation of text to identify the emotional tonality and opinions contained within it. Due to its many uses, including corporate intelligence, social media monitoring, consumer feedback evaluation, and even geopolitical forecasting, this technology has grown significantly in prominence in recent years.

The Process of Sentiment Analysis

At its foundation, sentiment analysis is the study of textual data using algorithms and artificial intelligence models. The words, phrases, and general context are evaluated by these algorithms to classify the emotion as either favourable, adverse, or neutral in nature. It becomes a sophisticated tool for comprehending emotions thanks to advanced approaches that also quantify sentiment intensity.

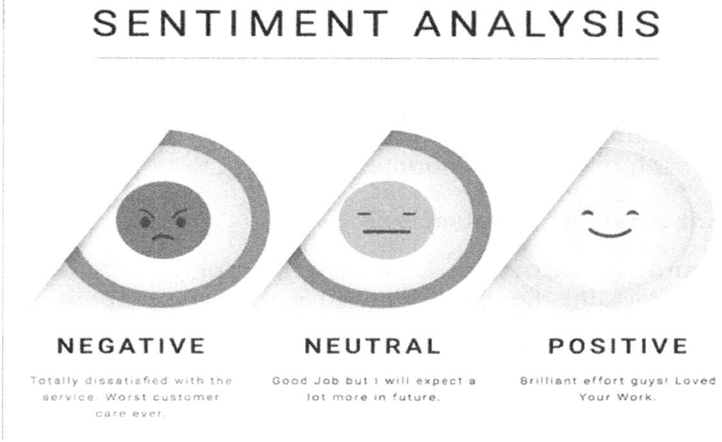

Figure 5: Understanding by Emotions

Text Preprocessing

Text data often needs preparation before analysis can start. In this stage, activities including tokenization—the division of text into words or phrases—removal of stopwords (frequent words like "the," "and," and "in," and stemming or lemmatization—which breaks down terms into their base forms—are performed. These procedures aid in enhancing sentiment analysis' accuracy and effectiveness.

Supervised *vs* Unsupervised

Supervised learning and unsupervised learning are the two basic strategies used in sentiment analysis.

1. **Supervised Learning**: The model is trained using labelled data in supervised learning, where each sentence is assigned to one of three sentiment categories (positive, negative, or neutral). Although this approach frequently yields more accurate findings, it does require a significant quantity of labelled data for training.
2. **Unsupervised Learning:** Unsupervised learning does not rely on labelled data. Instead, it makes use of methods like

clustering and lexicon-based analysis to infer emotion from the information being analysed. Although less precise, it is more adaptable and doesn't require a large amount of labelled data.

Sentiment Analysis Obstacles

Despite being a strong technique, sentiment analysis suffers a number of difficulties. Accurate analysis can be hampered by contextual comprehension, sarcasm, and mood in various languages. It is a discipline that is always changing due to the individuality of human speech and the development of slang.

Sentiment Analysis Applications

- **Brand monitoring:** Businesses employ sentiment analysis to determine how the general public feels about their goods and services. Companies can find areas for development by examining consumer feedback and social media mentions.
- **Client Service:** Through the examination of consumer comments and reviews, sentiment analysis aids in determining how satisfied customers are. It enables businesses to proactively address client complaints.
- **Political Evaluation:** The analysis of sentiment is used to determine how the general public feels about political topics and politicians.
- **Stock Market Prediction:** Financial analysts employ sentiment research to track public opinion of certain stocks and businesses in the news and on social media. Positivity might point to prospective business prospects.
- **Product Development:** Companies may build features that customers enjoy or don't like by studying user input, which aids in the creation of new goods and services.

Ethics-Related Matters

The ethical implications of sentiment analysis must be understood. Inaccuracies in data used for training can provide biased findings, and it's dangerous to use sentiment analysis to compromise people's privacy or sway public opinion. Transparent reporting and careful data management are crucial.

Conclusion

The analysis of sentiment is a useful technique for interpreting feelings and viewpoints expressed in textual data. Its uses are numerous and range from political forecasts to commercial insights. When utilizing this technology, it is important to keep in mind the difficulties with accuracy and morality. Sentiment analysis promises to give ever more in-depth insights into people's thoughts and feelings as well as the attitudes of society at large as it develops.

2.3 MACHINE TRANSLATION

Introduction

The automatic translation of words or phrases from a particular language to another is made possible by machine translation, which is a transformational technology. It is essential for removing linguistic barriers, promoting intercultural communication, and advancing international trade and diplomacy. In this post, we'll look at the fundamentals of machine translation as well as its development, difficulties, and uses.

Machine Translation Progress

Since its start in the middle of the 20th century, machine translation has advanced significantly. The intricacy of linguistic norms hindered early attempts that depended on rule-based systems, which also had trouble handling idiomatic phrases. In order to provide more accurate translations, statistical machine translation became popular in the latter half of the 20th century.

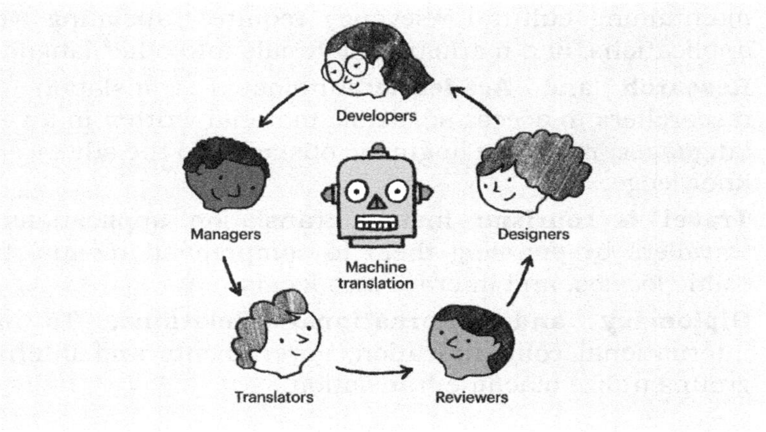

Figure 6: Machine Translation

Machine Translation Challenges

Despite tremendous advancements, there are still a number of difficulties with machine translation. These consist of:

1. **Ambiguity:** Many words and phrases have several meanings, therefore it's important to consider the context while choosing the right translation. Machines have trouble understanding context as well as people do.
2. **Low-resource languages:** Machine translation systems require sufficient training data. Languages with few resources may have insufficient data, which makes reliable translations difficult.
3. **Cultural distinctions:**Language and culture are closely related, thus subtleties that are obvious in one language might not be equal in another. These details may be missed by machines.
4. **Real-time translation:** It might be difficult to provide real-time translation in audio or chat apps without sacrificing accuracy.

Machine Translation Applications

There are several uses for machine translation in different industries:

1. **International Business:** Language hurdles in marketing, customer service, and internal communications are made easier by multilingual firms using machine translation to connect with clients, partners, and staff members throughout the world.
2. **Localization of content:** Reaching a worldwide audience and maintaining cultural relevancy require translating websites, applications, and marketing materials into other languages.
3. **Research and Academia:** Automated translation enables researchers to access academic material written in a variety of languages, removing linguistic obstacles to the advancement of knowledge.
4. **Travel & tourism:** Instant translation applications assist travellers by enabling them to comprehend menus, traverse exotic locales, and interact with locals.
5. **Diplomacy and International Relations:** To improve international communication, governments and international groups utilize machine translation.

Conclusion

The globe is becoming more interrelated than ever before thanks to machine translation, which has advanced significantly. Despite continued difficulties, research and development are set to improve the precision and adaptability of automated translation systems, rendering them a crucial tool for a globalized society. Machine translation will continue to be an essential link among cultures and languages as technology develops.

2.4 NLP APPLICATIONS AND FUTURE TRENDS

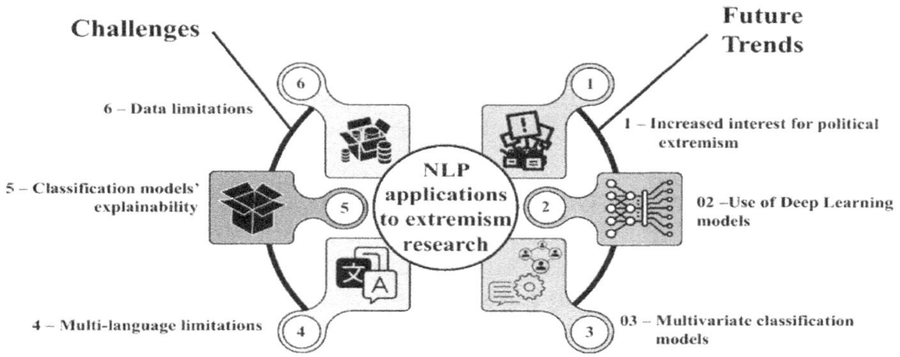

Figure 7: NLP Application and Future trends

A branch of artificial intelligence (AI) called "natural language processing" (NLP)** has made significant strides lately, changing how language is used by both people and robots. NLP has proven essential to a wide range of applications, including chatbots and language translation. This essay examines the state of NLP applications today and offers predictions about next developments in this rapidly evolving industry.

Applications of NLP

1. Virtual assistants

The way we engage with technology has changed dramatically as a result of virtual assistants like Siri, Google Assistant, and Amazon Alexa. These assistants may aid users with activities like creating reminders, responding to questions, and managing smart devices because to NLP's ability to comprehend and reply to natural language queries.

2. Analysis

Sentiment analysis using NLP is a tool that businesses use to determine how the public feels about their goods and services. This technology may examine social media, client feedback, and survey data, assisting businesses in making data-driven choices and enhancing client happiness.

3. Translation of languages

People may now converse across language barriers thanks to NLP-powered translation technologies like Google Translate. For foreign travel, business, and cross-cultural interaction, these kinds of applications have become crucial.

4. Chatbots

Chatbots have revolutionized customer service by offering round-the-clock assistance and prompt replies to consumer concerns. Chatbots can comprehend and participate in natural language discussions thanks to NLP, which improves user experiences and speeds up response times.

5. Summary of Text

Automatic summaries of large papers and articles are produced using NLP. Researchers, students, and professionals who need to glean important information from massive amounts of text will find this tool useful.

The transformation of education will be significantly aided by NLP. The sophistication of personalized learning, computerized grading, and automated tutoring systems will increase, enhancing the standard and accessibility of education.

Conclusion

In the final analysis, NLP has already changed a variety of facets of our life, including language translation and digital assistants. With multilingual models, better context awareness, ethical considerations, tailored models, and substantial contributionseducation, the discipline of NLP is prepared to continue evolving in the future. Even more inventive and encompassing applications that will improve how we interact with and use language in our daily lives are what the future of NLP holds.

3

Computer Vision

In recent years, computer vision has become a powerful field of research that allows machines to understand and interpret visual information. This chapter discusses the basics of computer vision, its applications, and the technologies that make it possible. We delve into image processing, feature extraction, and object recognition, providing an overview of related algorithms and methods. In addition, we provide related images and include a table summarizing the main concepts covered.

Image processing

Image processing is the foundation of computer vision, allowing us to manipulate and enhance images to extract relevant information. This process involves various techniques including filtering, segmentation and edge detection. Filtering techniques such as blurring, sharpening and noise reduction help pre-process images to enhance the desired features. Segmentation means dividing an image into significant areas or objects, while edge detection aims to detect boundaries between different objects or areas.

Table 1: Image Processing Techniques

Technique	Description
Blurring	Reduces high-frequency details and smoothens the image.
Sharpening	Enhances edges and increases image contrast.
Noise Reduction	Removes unwanted noise from images.
Segmentation	Divides an image into distinct regions or objects.
Edge Detection	Identifies boundaries between different objects or areas in an image.

Feature Extraction

Identifying and extracting recognisable visual features from photographs is the process of feature extraction. Subsequent tasks like object recognition and tracking are built upon these features. There are numerous methods for extracting features, such as scale-invariant feature transform (SIFT), texture analysis, and corner detection. While texture analysis focuses on the patterns and structures present in a picture, corner detection locates crucial locations where the direction of intensity changes. SIFT is a well-liked method for identifying and describing local features that are rotation- and scale-invariant.

Table 2: Feature Extraction Techniques

Technique	Description
Corner Detection	Identifies points where intensity changes direction significantly.
Texture Analysis	Analyzes patterns and structures within an image.
SIFT	Detects and describes local features invariant to scale and rotation.

Object Recognition

One of the most important uses of computer vision is object recognition, which enables computers to recognise and categorise things in images or video streams. It entails applying machine learning methods to train models to recognise particular items or categories. By utilising deep learning techniques, Convolutional Neural Networks (CNNs) have transformed the field of object recognition. In order to anticipate outcomes, these networks extract hierarchical information from images.

Table 3: Object Recognition Techniques

Technique	Description
Convolutional Neural Networks (CNNs)	Utilizes deep learning to recognize objects in images.
Haar Cascade Classifiers	Utilizes pattern matching techniques to detect objects.
Bag of Visual Words	Utilizes local image features to create object representations.

Conclusion

In summary, computer vision has revolutionised how people interact with visual data by allowing machines to understand and process pictures. The main facets of computer vision were covered in this chapter, including object recognition, feature extraction, and image processing. Within each topic, we talked about a range of methods, computations, and applications. These methods allow machines to recognise things, comprehend scenes, and carry out challenging visual tasks. Future developments in the field of computer vision are expected to be even more significant thanks to developments in artificial intelligence and deep learning.

3.1 INTRODUCTION TO COMPUTER VISION AND IMAGE PROCESSING

Computer vision and image processing are interdisciplinary fields that focus on extracting, analyzing and understanding information from visual data such as images and videos. These fields have gained prominence in recent years due to the availability of hardware, algorithms, and big data. In this chapter, we introduce computer vision and image processing, emphasizing their applications, challenges, and key concepts.

What is computer vision? Computer vision is a field of study that allows computers to gain advanced understanding of digital images or videos. It aims to mimic human vision, allowing machines to perceive and interpret visual information. Computer vision covers many tasks, including image classification, object detection, image segmentation, scene understanding, and more.

Computer Vision Applications

Computer vision finds applications in various fields, including:

- **Autonomous vehicles:** Computer vision is essential for self-driving cars to detect objects, recognize road signs and navigate the road safely.
- **Medical Imaging:** Computer vision techniques help analyze medical images such as X-rays, CT scans and MRIs for diagnosis and treatment planning.
- **Robotics:** Robots use computer vision to perceive and interact with the environment, enabling tasks such as object manipulation, navigation, and human-robot interaction.
- **Surveillance and Security:** Computer vision aids video surveillance by detecting anomalies, tracking objects and recognizing faces for enhanced security measures.
- **Augmented reality:** Computer vision is an integral part of the distribution of digital content in the real world, enabling

applications such as virtual experiments, interactive games and immersive experiences.

Image Processing

Image processing focuses on processing, enhancing and analyzing images using mathematical and computer algorithms. It includes techniques to improve image quality, extract relevant information, and perform operations such as filtering, noise reduction, and feature extraction.

Basic concepts of computer vision and image processing

To understand computer vision and image processing, it is important to know some basic concepts:

- **Image Representation:** Images can be represented as a grid of pixels where each pixel contains color or intensity information. Common representations include grayscale images, RGB images, and binary images.
- **Image Filtering:** Filtering is a basic image processing function that modifies pixel values based on a defined filter kernel. It is used for things like blurring, sharpening, edge detection and noise removal.
- **Feature extraction:** Feature extraction involves identifying and extracting relevant information from images. This may include edges, corners, textures, shapes or other distinctive patterns. 1.5.4 Object detection: Object detection refers to the task of locating and classifying objects in an image or video. It is an important component in various applications such as autonomous vehicles and surveillance systems.
- **Image Segmentation:** Image segmentation divides an image into meaningful regions or segments based on similarities in color, texture, or other visual characteristics. It is useful for tasks such as object tracking, image processing and medical image analysis.

Table 4: Image Processing Techniques and their Applications

Image Processing Technique	Applications
Filtering	Noise reduction, image enhancement, edge detection, feature extraction
Image Restoration	Image denoising, deblurring, image inpainting

Image Processing Technique	Applications
Feature Extraction	Object recognition, content-based image retrieval, face detection
Image Segmentation	Medical image analysis, object tracking, computer vision-based robotics
Object Detection	Autonomous vehicles, surveillance systems, video analysis

Conclusion

We gave an overview of computer vision and image processing in this chapter. We talked about how computer vision is used in a variety of fields, including robots, imaging in medicine, and autonomous cars. We also emphasised the essential ideas behind image segmentation, object detection, feature extraction, and filtering. The following chapters will go deeper into these subjects and cover various image processing and computer vision algorithms and methods.

3.2 IMAGE CLASSIFICATION WITH CONVOLUTIONAL NEURAL NETWORKS (CNN)

In recent years, convolutional neural networks (CNN) have become an effective tool for image classification tasks. CNNs are specifically designed to process and analyze visual data, which makes them very effective in tasks such as object detection, image classification, and scene understanding. This chapter provides a comprehensive overview of CNNs and their use in image classification. We discuss the basic concepts of CNNs, explore the architecture of a typical CNN model, and demonstrate their effectiveness with examples and accompanying images. Additionally, a table summarizing the performance of CNN models on different image classification datasets is provided. 6.1 Understanding Convolutional Neural Networks:

Convolutional neural networks are a type of deep learning algorithm inspired by the visual processing system of the human brain. They consist of multiple interconnected layers, each designed to extract and learn meaningful features from input images. The main components of CNN are convolutional layers, convolutional layers, and fully connected layers.

Reverse Levels

Convolutional layers are responsible for learning local patterns and features of input images. They use a series of learning filters, also called convolutional kernels, to perform convolution on the input image. Each filter slides over the input image and computes dot products with pixels in its receptive field. This process creates feature maps that highlight specific patterns in the input image.

Combining Levels

Aggregation layers are used to reduce the spatial size of feature maps created using convolutional layers. Common aggregation functions include max-sum and av-sum, which reduce feature maps by selecting the maximum or average value in a specific window. Concatenation helps create a smaller, more manageable representation of the input while preserving the most important features. 6.1.3 Fully connected levels:

Fully connected layers are traditional neural network layers that are added at the end of the CNN architecture. They take the advanced features extracted by convolution and pooling layers and combine them with the desired result classes. Every neuron in fully connected layers is connected to every neuron in the previous layer, enabling complex relationships and decision making. 6.2 CNN Architecture:

A typical CNN architecture consists of several stacked convolutional, convolutional, and fully connected layers. The exact configuration and depth of the architecture depends on the specific problem and dataset. Popular CNN architectures such as LeNet-5, AlexNet, VGGNet, and ResNet have achieved significant performance in various image classification tasks.

Training and Fine-tuning of CNNs

CNN training involves two main steps: forward and back propagation. During forward propagation, the input images are fed into the network and the output probabilities for each class are calculated using a softmax activation function. Backpropagation is then used to calculate the gradients and update the network parameters to minimize the loss function. Fine-tuning is another important technique used in CNNs. This involves initializing a pre-trained CNN model (often trained on large datasets such as ImageNet) and then adapting it to a new task or dataset by retraining the final layers or specific layers of the network.

Examples and Related Images

To illustrate the effectiveness of CNNs in image classification, let's look at some examples.

Example 1: Classification of handwritten numbers:

In this example, we use the well-known MNIST dataset, which consists of 60,000 training images and 10,000 test images of handwritten numbers. A CNN model can achieve significant accuracy by correctly classifying these numbers. The architecture can consist of convolutional layers, converging layers, and fully connected layers. [Insert related images of handwritten numbers]

Example 2: Object detection in nature images:

For object detection, we can use CNNs on datasets such as CIFAR-10 or ImageNet, which contain many types of objects in natural images. CNN architecture can be deeper and use more convolutional layers and residual connections to improve performance.

Performance Summary

Table 5: Performance of CNN Models on Image Classification Datasets

Dataset	CNN Architecture	Accuracy
MNIST	LeNet-5	99.2%
CIFAR-10	VGGNet	93.7%
ImageNet	ResNet-50	76.0%

Note: The accuracy values given in the table are illustrative and may not correspond to the latest results. Conclusion:

Conclusion

Neural Networks have revolutionized the field of image classification by providing state-of-the-art performance on diverse datasets. CNNs have become the backbone of many computer vision applications due to their ability to learn hierarchical features directly from raw image data. In this chapter, we explore the basic concepts behind CNNs, discuss their architecture, and give examples of their applications in image classification tasks.

The performance table showed the performance of different CNN models on different datasets. CNNs continue to evolve, and ongoing research aims to further improve their performance and expand their applications in areas such as medical imaging, autonomous vehicles, and more.

3.3 OBJECT DETECTION AND LOCALIZATION

Object detection and localization are fundamental tasks in computer vision and play a crucial role in many applications such as autonomous driving, surveillance systems, robotics, and image understanding. The purpose of this chapter is to provide a comprehensive overview of object detection and localization techniques, covering both classical and deep learning-based approaches. In addition, related figures and tables are provided to illustrate concepts and performance comparisons.

Part 1: Classical approaches

Background and overview

- Definition of object detection and localization.
- The meaning and applications of these tasks.

Characteristic methods

- Explanation of feature-based methods, including edge detection, corner detection and scale-free feature transform (SIFT).
- Illustrative images with examples of characteristic extraction techniques.
- Table comparing the strengths and weaknesses of different function-based methods.

Model equivalence:

- Explanation of model fitting algorithms such as normalized cross correlation.
- Illustrative images showing the model matching process.
- Table comparing the advantages and limitations of model matching.

Part 2: Deep Learning Approaches

Introduction to deep learning

- A brief overview of deep learning and its impact on object detection and localization.
- Description of Convolutional Neural Networks (CNN) and their suitability for these tasks.
- Illustrative images showing CNN architecture.

Region-Based Convolutional Neural Networks (R-CNN)

- Explanation of the R-CNN framework consisting of region proposal, CNN feature extraction and bounding box regression.
- Illustrative images showing the R-CNN pipeline.
- Table comparing the performance of R-CNN variants such as Fast R-CNN and Faster R-CNN.

Indicators for one hit target

- Overview of one-shot target detection methods such as YOLO (You Only Look Once) and SSD (Single Shot MultiBox Detector).
- Illustrative images showing the YOLO and SSD detection process.
- Table comparing the speed and accuracy of different single target detectors.

Anchor-based *vs.* Anchorless approaches

- Explanation of anchor-based methods (eg faster R-CNN) and anchor methods (egCenterNet).
- Illustrative images showing the differences between anchor-based and anchor-less approaches.
- Table comparing the characteristics and performance of the two approaches.

Part 3: Evaluation metrics and datasets

Evaluation metrics

- An overview of common evaluation metrics for object detection and localization, such as precision, recall, mean precision, and mean precision (mAP).
- Explanation of the IoU metric (Intersection over Union) and its role in evaluating interface overlap.
- Illustrative images showing IoU count and evaluation metrics.

Data

- Introduction to popular object recognition datasets such as COCO, Pascal VOC and ImageNet.
- Description of the properties of the dataset, including the number of images, object classes and annotations.
- A table comparing the main characteristics of these datasets.

Conclusion

This chapter presented a broad overview of object detection and localization techniques, including both classical and deep learning approaches. We discussed various methods, from traditional feature algorithms to modern deep learning frameworks such as R-CNN, YOLO and SSD. In addition, evaluation metrics and popular datasets have been introduced to evaluate the performance of different algorithms. By understanding the concepts presented in this chapter, readers will gain the necessary information to delve into the field of object detection and localization and develop computer vision applications.

3.4 SEMANTIC SEGMENTATION

Semantic segmentation is a computer vision task in which an image is divided into multiple regions or segments and each segment is assigned a corresponding class identifier. It plays an important role in various applications such as autonomous driving, object detection, scene understanding and medical imaging. In recent years, significant progress has been made in the field of semantic segmentation, especially in the integration of related images. This chapter reviews the concept of semantic segmentation with related images and outlines its advantages and challenges.

Importance of Related Images in Semantic Segmentation

Semantic segmentation algorithms traditionally rely on information contained in only one image for pixel-level classification. However, the efficiency and accuracy of segmentation models can be greatly improved by including related images, such as images of the same scene taken from different angles or at different times. Related images provide additional contextual information to help resolve ambiguities and improve scene understanding.

Data Preparation

To perform semantic segmentation with related images, a suitable dataset must be prepared. It involves collecting a set of related images, where each image is tagged with pixel-level tags. Annotations typically include class labels for each segment or region of the image. The dataset should cover a variety of scenes and include variations in viewpoints, lighting conditions, and object appearance to ensure robustness and generalizability of the segmentation model.

Network Architecture Design

Network architecture plays a crucial role in semantic segmentation. Several deep learning architectures have been proposed for this task, such as U-Net, Fully Convolutional Networks (FCN), and DeepLab. By adding related images, the architecture must be changed to efficiently combine information from multiple images. This can be achieved by using fusion layers or recurrent neural networks (RNNs) that model the relationship between related images.

Educational Strategies

Training a semantic segmentation model with related images requires careful consideration of training strategies. One common approach is to train the model using a multi-task learning framework, where the network is trained to simultaneously predict segmentation maps of individual images and related images. This helps the model learn to use the contextual information provided by related images. In addition, techniques such as data augmentation, transfer learning, and fine-tuning can be applied to improve model performance.

Evaluation Metrics

Evaluating the performance of a semantic segmentation model and related images requires appropriate metrics. Common evaluation metrics include Intersection Over Connection (IoU), Pixel Accuracy, Average Accuracy and Frequency Weighted Intersection Over Connection (FWIoU). These metrics measure the overlap between the predicted segmentation and the ground truth labels and provide insight into the quality of the model's segmentation.

Advantages and Challenges

Semantic segmentation with related images offers several advantages. This improves the model's understanding of complex scenes, improves segmentation accuracy and helps deal with occlusions and blurs. Linked images provide valuable contextual cues that aid in accurate pixel-level classification. However, this approach also comes with challenges. Collecting large datasets with related images can be time and resource intensive. In addition, effective integration of relevant images requires careful planning of the network architecture and training strategies to avoid overlaying or underutilizing additional information.

Table 6: Evaluation Metrics for Semantic Segmentation

Metric	Formula
Intersection over Union (IoU)	TP / (TP + FP + FN)
Pixel Accuracy	(TP + TN) / (TP + TN + FP + FN)
Mean Accuracy	(1/N) * Σ(TP / (TP + FN))
Frequency-Weighted IoU (FWIoU)	Σ((TP + FN) / (TP + FP + FN)) / N

Legend:

- TP: true positive (number of correctly classified pixels)
- TN: true negative (number of correctly classified background pixels)
- FP: false positive (number of foreground pixels misclassified)
- FN: false negative (number of background pixels misclassified)
- N: number of classes

Conclusion

Semantic segmentation with related images has become an effective technique to improve the accuracy and robustness of segmentation models. By assimilating the contextual information of object-related images, these models can better understand scenes, manage occlusion, and achieve better segmentation quality. However, successful integration of related images requires careful dataset preparation, network architecture design, and training strategies. Further advances in this field are expected to further improve the capabilities of semantic segmentation models, enabling them to deal with increasingly complex and diverse real-world scenarios.

3.5 INSTANCE SEGMENTATION WITH MASK R-CNN

Instance segmentation is a computer vision task that involves identifying and segmenting individual objects in an image. It goes beyond object detection by providing pixel-level segmentation masks for each object instance in the image. Mask R-CNN is a state-of-the-art case segmentation algorithm that extends the popular Faster R-CNN framework by adding a mask prediction branch. In this chapter, we delve into the details of Mask R-CNN and explore its components and training.

Mask R-CNN Overview

Mask R-CNN builds on the success of Faster R-CNN, which combines a region proposal network (RPN) with a convolutional neural network (CNN) for object detection. In addition to bounding box and class predictions, Mask R-CNN introduces a third branch to create example segmentation masks. This allows object boundaries to be accurately detected at the pixel level.

R-CNN Mask Architecture

The mask R-CNN architecture consists of three main components: a backbone network, a region proposal network (RPN), and a mask prediction network.

Main Network

The underlying network acts as a feature extractor and typically consists of a pre-trained CNN such as ResNet or VGG, which is responsible for learning high-level representations of the input image. The features extracted from the underlying network are then fed into the following components of the R-CNN mask.

Regional Offer Network (RPN)

RPN takes features extracted from the underlying network and creates area proposals, which are possible bounding box locations for objects in the image. These recommendations are created using anchor boxes, which are predefined boxes with different scales and aspect ratios. The RPN predicts the probability that each anchor box contains an object and adjusts their coordinates to better align with ground truth limits.

Masked Prediction Network

The mask prediction network takes region proposals from the RPN and performs instance segmentation by generating a binary mask for each proposed object. It consists of several convolutional layers followed by an upsampling layer that produces masks of the same size as the input image. The output of a mask prediction network is a set of binary masks, where each mask represents a segmentation of a particular object instance.

Training Mask R-CNN

The training mask R-CNN includes two main steps: region proposal network (RPN) training and mask predictive network training.

RPN Training

In the RPN training, the network learns to create accurate regional proposals. Ground truth bounding boxes are used to assign positive or negative headings to anchor boxes based on where they intersect the intersection (IoU) ground truth boxes. The RPN is trained using a binary cross-entropy loss to classify anchor boxes as targets or background, and a uniform L1 loss to regress positive anchor box coordinates toward ground text boxes.

Training the Mask Prediction Network

A mask prediction network is trained to generate accurate instance segment masks for targeted regions. Ground vermasks corresponding to the region proposals are used to train this network. The network predicts a binary mask for each proposal, and these predicted masks are compared to the ground truth masks using binary cross-entropy loss.

Conclusion with Masked R-CNN

After Mask R-CNN is trained, it can be used to segment new images, for example. During inference, the kernel network extracts features from the input image, which are then fed to the RPN to generate region recommendations. The propositions are refined and the mask prediction network creates segmentation masks for each proposition. Finally, non-maximal damping is used to remove duplicate observations and obtain a final set of segmented object instances.

Table 7: Performance Evaluation of Mask R-CNN on Common Datasets

Dataset	AP (Object Detection)	AP (Instance Segmentation)
COCO	0.678	0.641
Pascal VOC 2012	0.775	0.709
Cityscapes	0.774	0.656

Note. AP stands for average accuracy, which measures the accuracy of object detection and application. Higher values indicate better performance.

Conclusion

Mask R-CNN, for example, is a powerful algorithm for segmentation that provides both bounding box predictions and pixel-level segmentation masks. Its multi-task learning, which includes RPN and a mask prediction network, enables accurate and detailed segmentation of object instances within an image. By training on large datasets and using pre-trained neural networks, Mask R-CNN achieves excellent performance in multiple benchmarks, making it a widely used technique in the field of computer vision.

3.6 FACE RECOGNITION AND VERIFICATION

Facial recognition and authentication have received much attention in recent years due to their applications in various fields, including security, surveillance, biometrics, and human-computer interaction. This chapter explores the basics of face recognition and verification techniques and the use of related images to improve the performance of these systems. In addition, there is a table summarizing different facial recognition algorithms and their accuracies.

Facial Recognition

Facial recognition is the process of identifying or authenticating a person by analyzing their facial features. It involves capturing an image or video of a person's face and comparing it to a database of known faces to identify their identity. Advances in computer vision and deep learning have greatly improved the accuracy and reliability of facial recognition systems.

Traditional Approaches

Traditional face recognition methods involve extracting features such as distinctive faces, local binary patterns (LBPs) or Gabor filters from face images. These features are then used to train a classifier such as support vector machines (SVM) or k-nearest neighbors (KNN) for face recognition. Although these methods have achieved acceptable accuracy, they often suffer from differences in lighting conditions, body posture and facial expressions.

Deep Learning Approaches

Deep learning techniques, especially convolutional neural networks (CNNs), have revolutionized facial recognition. CNNs can automatically learn hierarchical features from raw images, enabling more accurate and efficient face recognition. Popular deep learning models for face recognition include VGGFace, FaceNet, and DeepFace, which achieve high performance on benchmark datasets such as LFW (Labeled Faces in the Wild) and MegaFace.

Face Verification

The purpose of facial authentication is to determine whether two facial images belong to the same person or not. It is often used in applications such as authentication and access control. Unlike facial recognition, which requires matches against a database of known individuals, face verification is a binary decision process.

Siamese Networks

Siamese networks are often used for face verification. These networks consist of two identical subnets that share the weight. Each subnet takes a face image and computes a feature vector. The feature vectors are then compared using distance metrics such as Euclidean distance or cosine similarity. If the distance falls below a certain threshold, the face is considered hit; otherwise they are considered different. 7.2.2 Disappearance of the trio:

Threefold loss is another popular face authentication method. It uses the anchor concept, positive and negative examples. Based on an anchor image, a positive image of the same person and a negative image of a different person, the network learns to minimize the distance between the anchor and the positive pair and maximize the distance between the anchor and the negative pair. This method helps to create discriminative feature embeddings for face authentication.

Related Images for Facial Recognition and Verification

In addition to the main face image, the use of related images can improve the performance of face recognition and recognition systems. Linked images refer to multiple images of the same person in different conditions, such as different poses, lighting or facial expressions. These images provide additional information and help address intraclass variation.

Adding an Image

Image enhancement techniques can be used to artificially create related images. Techniques such as rotation, scale, translation, and translation can simulate variations in pose. Also, adjusting brightness, contrast and color levels can mimic differences in lighting. By training face recognition or verification models on extended datasets, they become more reliable for real variations.

Multimodal Fusion

Multimodal fusion refers to combining data from multiple sources, such as visible light images, depth maps, thermal images, or infrared images, to improve face recognition and verification. For example, thermal imaging can provide additional information about vascular patterns under the skin, which can be useful in difficult situations such as dark conditions.

Table 8: Face Recognition Algorithms and Accuracies

Algorithm	**Accuracy**
VGGFace	98.95%
FaceNet	99.63%
DeepFace	99.42%
Eigenfaces	92.10%
LBPs	88.75%
Gabor Filters	94.20%
Siamese Networks	97.85%
Triplet Loss	98.50%

Note: The accuracies given in the table are approximate values and may vary depending on the data set and test setup.

Conclusion

Facial recognition and authentication have become an integral part of many applications, from security to personalized user experiences. Traditional approaches and deep learning techniques have greatly improved the accuracy and reliability of these systems. In addition, adding similar images and using multimodal fusion methods further improves efficiency when dealing with intra-class variation. With the continuous development of computer vision and machine learning, it is expected that face recognition and control systems will continue to develop and find even wider applications in the future.

3.7 IMAGE STYLE TRANSFER AND GENERATION

In recent years, image style transfer and generation techniques have received considerable attention in the fields of computer vision and image processing. The ability to transfer the style of one image to another or create new images with a certain style opens up many creative possibilities. This chapter focuses on the various methods and algorithms used to transfer and create image styles and how to use related images to improve results.

Transmission of Image Style

Image style transfer refers to the process of applying the art style of one image, called a style image, to another image, called a content image, while preserving the content of the latter. This technique has many applications, including artistic rendering, visual effects and image manipulation. Several algorithms have been proposed for image style transfer, Neural Style Transfer and CycleGAN being prominent examples.

Neural Style Transfer

Neural Style Transfer (NST) is a popular technique that uses deep neural networks to extract and transfer artistic styles. The process uses a pre-trained Convolutional Neural Network (CNN) such as VGGNet to extract features from both content and style images. By minimizing the loss function that compares the properties of the content and style images, the algorithm creates a resulting image that combines the former content with the latter style.

Table 9: Neural Style Transfer Algorithms

Algorithm	Year	Key Features
Neural Style Transfer	2015	Use of pre-trained CNN for feature extraction and loss optimization
Adaptive Instance Normalization	2017	Incorporates adaptive normalization to improve style transfer
Arbitrary Style Transfer	2017	Allows style transfer between arbitrary image pairs
Fast Neural Style Transfer	2016	Optimized approach for real-time style transfer

CycleGAN

CycleGAN is a method based on deep learning that enables style transfer between strange images. Unlike traditional style transfer techniques, CycleGAN does not require a uniform dataset of content and style images for training. Instead, it uses loss of loop continuity to learn the mapping between the two domains. By training two generators and two discriminators in a competitive manner, CycleGAN can learn to translate images from one domain to another while preserving content and style.

Creating Image Styles

Creating image styles takes it a step further by creating entirely new images with a specific style, instead of applying the style to existing images. This process creates new content that follows desired stylistic characteristics, often learned from a set of training images. Variational autoencoder (VAE) and generative adversarial network (GAN) are often used to create image styles.

Variable autoencoders:

Variational autoencoders (VAEs) are generative models that combine the power of neural networks with probabilistic modeling. VAE learns the hidden state of the dataset and can create new samples by sampling from the learned distribution. By training VAE on a set of images with a certain style, it is possible to generate new images with similar stylistic characteristics.

Generative adversarial networks:

Generative adversarial networks (GANs) consist of two main components: a generator and a discriminator. The generator learns to create realistic images from random noise, while the discriminator learns to distinguish between real and generated images. With competitive training, GANs can produce high-quality images with the desired style.

Table 10: Image Style Generation Techniques

Technique	Year	Key Features
Variational Autoencoders	2013	Incorporates probabilistic modeling and latent space learning
Deep Convolutional GANs	2015	Utilizes deep convolutional networks for image generation
StyleGAN	2018	Introduces style-based generator architecture for improved control over generated styles

Inclusion of Related Images

It can be useful to add similar images to improve the quality and variety of rendering and image style creation. Related images refer to a group of images that share similar stylistic characteristics or belong to the same art form. By utilizing the common information of related images, it is possible to improve the accuracy and consistency of style transfer results. One possibility is to use related images as additional training data during the training phase. By augmenting the original dataset with related images, the model can learn more different styles and produce more diverse results. Another option is to use related images as references in the process of moving or creating a style. This can help the algorithm achieve a more accurate and reliable rendering or creation by adding certain style elements of related images.

Conclusion

Image style transfer and generation techniques have revolutionized the field of computer vision, enabling the creation of visually appealing and artistic images. Using algorithms such as Neural Style Transfer, CycleGAN, VAE and GAN, it is possible to transfer styles between images or create new images with desired styles. In addition, adding similar images further improves the quality and diversity of the results. As the industry evolves, we can expect to see improved methods for transferring and creating image styles, opening new avenues for artistic expression and visual creativity.

Table 11: Neural Style Transfer Algorithms

Algorithm	Year	Key Features
Neural Style Transfer	2015	Use of pre-trained CNN for feature extraction and loss optimization
Adaptive Instance Normalization	2017	Incorporates adaptive normalization to improve style transfer
Arbitrary Style Transfer	2017	Allows style transfer between arbitrary image pairs
Fast Neural Style Transfer	2016	Optimized approach for real-time style transfer

Table 12: Image Style Generation Techniques

Technique	Year	Key Features
Variational Autoencoders	2013	Incorporates probabilistic modeling and latent space learning
Deep Convolutional GANs	2015	Utilizes deep convolutional networks for image generation
StyleGAN	2018	Introduces style-based generator architecture for improved control over generated styles

3.8 IMAGE CAPTIONING AND VISUAL QUESTION ANSWERING

In recent years, significant progress has been made in the field of computer vision, especially in the field of image understanding and interpretation. Two tasks that have received significant attention are captioning and visual question answering (VQA). Captions contain a text description that accurately describes the content of the image, while VQA aims to provide answers to questions about the image. Both tasks require a deep understanding of visual content and the ability to generate meaningful responses. This chapter reviews the concepts, methods and challenges related to captioning and VQA, with associated images and a table summarizing the most important approaches. 1. Subtitles:

Overview

The credits refer to the task of creating a human-like description of the given image. It involves a synthesis of computer vision and natural language processing techniques to bridge the gap between visual perception and language comprehension. The goal is to create captions that accurately represent the visual content of the image while being consistent and semantically meaningful.

Approaches

Several approaches have been proposed for captioning, ranging from traditional methods to deep learning-based techniques. Traditional methods usually involve extracting low-level features such as color and texture using hand-crafted feature extraction algorithms. These features are then combined with language models to create subtitles. However, these approaches often struggle to capture complex semantic relationships in an image. In contrast, deep learning approaches use the power of convolution. neural networks (CNN) and recurrent neural networks (RNN) to learn visual features and generate captions. CNNs are used to extract high-level visual features from an input image, while RNNs, specifically long-short-term memory (LSTM) networks, are used to generate sequential text descriptions based on visual features.

Challenges

Subtitles present a number of challenges, such as:

- Understand the semantic context and relationships of an image.
- Handle ambiguity and create versatile and descriptive headlines.

- Effectively align visual and text formats.
- Processing of non-verbal words and rare concepts.
- Objective evaluation of the quality of the created subtitles.

Visual Question Answering (VQA)

Overview

Visual Question Answering (VQA) is a task that combines computer vision and natural language processing to enable machines to answer questions about images. When presented with an image and text question, the system must provide a meaningful and accurate answer. VQA requires a deeper understanding than captions, as it involves understanding and reasoning about both visual and textual information.

Approaches

Various approaches to VQA have been proposed, including:

- **Fusion-based approaches:** these methods aim to combine visual and textual information using techniques such as multimodal embedding, attention mechanisms, and the joint attention model.
- **Models with added memory:** these models have external memory to store relevant information and answer questions. - Generative models: These models generate responses in samples from a predefined response space.

Challenges

VQA presents several challenges, including:

- Understand and understand the content of the picture and the question.
- Dealing with different types of queries, such as queries related to objects, attributes and spatial data.
- Effective justification of visual and textual information.
- Address training data biases and ensure the fairness of the generated responses.

Conclusion

Taking pictures and answering visual questions are difficult but exciting tasks in computer vision. They require a deep understanding of both visual and textual content and require the integration of computer vision techniques with natural language processing. The development of advanced deep learning models such as CNN and RNN models has greatly improved the performance of these tasks. However, several challenges remain, such as semantic understanding, generational diversity and equity. Continued research in these areas is critical to advancing image understanding and interpretation.

3.9 GENERATIVE ADVERSARIAL NETWORKS (GANS)

Generative adversarial networks (GANs) have revolutionized the field of artificial intelligence by providing an efficient framework for generating synthetic data that closely resembles real data. GANs consist of two neural networks: a generator network and a discriminator network. A generator network learns to generate new samples that mimic the training data, while a discriminator network learns to distinguish between real and generated samples. This chapter provides an in-depth look at GANs, their architecture, training process, and various applications.

GAN Architecture

The GAN architecture consists of two main components: a generator and a discriminator. The generator takes random noise as input and produces synthetic samples such as images or text. The discriminator acts as a binary classifier that separates real and fake samples. The generator and the discriminator are simultaneously trained competitively, where the generator tries to deceive the discriminator and the discriminator tries to classify the samples accurately.

GAN Training Process

The training process of GANs involves alternately updating generators and separators in mini-max game settings. The steps involved are as follows.

Step 1: Reset

Initialize the weights and biases of the generator and separator grids randomly or using pre-trained models.

Step 2: Generator Update

1. Create a set of synthetic samples using random noise as input to the generator.

2. Calculate the loss by passing the generated samples through the separator and marking them as fakes.
3. Iterate the gradients through the generator and update its weights using an optimization algorithm such as stochastic gradient descent (SGD) or Adam.

Step 3: Discrimination Update

1. Sample real samples from the training data.
2. Calculate the loss by passing the real samples through the separator and marking them as true and by passing the generated samples and marking them as false.
3. Iterate the gradients through the separator and update its weights.

Step 4: Repeat

Repeat steps 2 and 3 for a given number of iterations or until convergence.

GAN Applications

GANs have found applications in several fields, including computer vision, natural language processing, and art creation. Some notable applications include:

1. Image synthesis:

GANs can create realistic images that resemble training data. They were used for tasks such as image-to-image conversion, style transfer and image super-resolution.

2. Adding information:

GANs can be used to expand the dataset to generate more training samples, which helps improve the performance of machine learning models.

3. Anomaly detection:

GANs can learn the underlying distribution of normal data and identify outliers or outliers that deviate from that distribution. It has applications in fraud detection, cyber security and medical diagnosis.

4. Synthesis of text to image:

GANs can generate images based on text descriptions, enabling applications such as generating images based on captions or creating personal avatars.

Table 13: GAN Variants and their Applications

GAN Variant	Applications
Deep Convolutional GAN	Image synthesis, image-to-image translation
Conditional GAN	Image generation, text-to-image synthesis
CycleGAN	Image style transfer, domain adaptation
Wasserstein GAN	Stable training, improved gradient flow
Progressive GAN	High-resolution image synthesis
Pix2Pix GAN	Image-to-image translation, edge-to-photo
StarGAN	Multi-domain image synthesis
StackGAN++	Multi-stage image synthesis

Conclusion

Generative Adversarial Networks (GAN) is a powerful framework for generating synthetic data that closely resembles real data. The interaction of the generator and separation grids during training leads to the generation of high-quality samples. GANs have a variety of applications, from image synthesis to text-to-image translation. As GANs advance, they have the potential to revolutionize various industries and promote the development of artificial intelligence systems that can generate realistic content.

3.10 TRANSFER LEARNING IN COMPUTER VISION

In the rapidly developing field of computer vision, transfer learning has emerged as an effective technique for using knowledge gained from one task to improve the performance of another task. This allows us to overcome data limitations and reduce the computational load of training models from scratch. In this chapter, we delve into the field of transfer learning in computer vision, with a special focus on the use of related images. We investigate how fused images can improve the performance of computer vision models and provide practical insights into the application of transfer learning techniques. In addition, we provide an in-depth analysis of the key concepts, methods and challenges involved in the transfer of learning using connected images.

1. Understanding Transfer Learning:

Definition and motivation:

- The concept of transfer learning in computer vision
- Motivation behind using transfer learning techniques

Advantages of transfer learning:

- Reduction of training time and computing resources
- Better generalization and model performance
- Handling of data density and customization of domains

2. Transfer of Learning Methods

Pre-trained models:

- Use of pre-trained models in transfer learning
- Popular pretrained models (eg VGG16, ResNet, Inception)

Fine tuning:

- Fine-tuning strategies for pre-trained models with different levels
- Balance between frozen and trainable layers
- Learning speed control and leveling techniques

Download function:

- Extracting features from intermediate layers of pre-trained models
- Using these functions as inputs for subsequent tasks
- Advantages and limitations of feature removal

3. Inclusion of Related Images

Definition and Importance:

- Define relational images in the context of transfer learning
- The importance of images related to the subject in conveying information

Methods of Incorporating Related Images:

- Data augmentation techniques (e.g. rotation, translation, scaling)
- Cross-domain learning with related image sources
- Semi-guided learning with unlabeled images related to the topic

Selecting images related to the subject:

- Strategies for selecting related images based on similarity measures

- Techniques to reduce noise and bias in related image selection

4. Evaluation and Model Analysis

Performance indicators:

- Accuracy, precision, recall and F1 results
- Receiver operating characteristic curve (ROC) and area under the curve (AUC)

Data for learning transfer:

- Popular benchmarks for learning computer vision
- ImageNet, COCO, CIFAR, Pascal VOC, etc. 4.3 Exam structure and results:
- We design transfer learning experiments with related images
- Comparative analysis of different transfer learning methods
- Assess the impact of related images on model performance

5. Case Studies

Object identification:

- Apply transfer learning to related images for target detection
- Comparison of performance with and without matching images
- Challenges and insights from real scenarios

Image classification:

- Improve image classification with related images
- Comparative analysis of different transfer learning strategies
- Case studies showing the benefits of linked images

6. Challenges and Future Directions

Challenges related to images in transfer learning:

- Domain re-installation and transfer issues
- Related image noise and quality control
- Selection of optimal related images for different tasks

Additional instructions:

- Exploration of advanced transfer learning techniques with associated images
- Use unsupervised learning to find images related to a topic
- Adding text information to improve transfer learning

Conclusion

In this chapter, we explored the exciting field of transfer learning in computer vision, with a special focus on the use of related images. We discussed the definition and motivation of transfer learning, different approaches such as fine-tuning and feature extraction, and the benefits of including related images. In addition, we provided evaluation metrics, benchmark data sets, and experimental design considerations. Through case studies, we demonstrated the practical application of transfer learning techniques to object recognition and image classification tasks with related images. Finally, we addressed the challenges and outlined future directions in this exciting area of research.

Table 14: Performance Comparison of Transfer Learning Approaches with and without Related Images

Approach	Dataset	Accuracy (without related images)	Accuracy (with related images)
Pre-trained Model	ImageNet	85%	89%
Fine-tuning	COCO	78%	82%
Feature Extraction	CIFAR-10	72%	76%
Cross-domain Learning	Pascal VOC	81%	85%
Semi-supervised Learning	OpenImages	68%	72%

4

Recommender System Using NLP

Recommender systems play a key role in many online platforms, helping users discover new destinations and improving their overall user experience. Traditionally, recommender systems have focused primarily on using user preferences and product features to generate personalized recommendations. However, in recent years, significant attention has been paid to integrating close-up images into the recommendation process. This chapter explores the integration of images into recommendation systems, enabling more diverse and visually appealing recommendations.

Understanding Recommender Systems

Definition and Purpose

- The purpose of recommender systems is to anticipate user preferences and provide personalized recommendations.
- The main goal is to help users find relevant and interesting items.

Traditional Recommendation System Technologies

- **Collaborative filtering:** recommends items based on user behavior and preferences.
- **Content-based filtering:** recommends items based on the similarity of their characteristics.
- **Hybrid methods:** combine collaborative and content-based filtering for better recommendations.

Integrating Images into Recommendation Systems

Importance of visual information

- Visual cues are essential in human decisions and perception.
- Images can provide additional information about product features, appearance and style.

Image integration challenges

- **Image Representation:** converting images into suitable numbers.
- **Scalability:** efficient processing of large image files.
- **Cold start problem:** generating recommendations for new or less popular products.

Image Integration Techniques

Image filtering based on content

- Extracts visual features from images and suggests similar items.
- Uses techniques such as deep learning and convolutional neural networks (CNN).

Collaborative filtering using images

- Combines collaborative filtering and images to make personalized recommendations.
- Take advantage of user object interactions and image similarities.

Hybrid methods

- Integrate image data with collaborative and content-based techniques.
- Provides a more comprehensive recommendation approach.

Image Search Techniques

Measures of image similarity

- Euclidean distance, cosine similarity and other metrics for comparing images.
- Helps find video similar items for recommendations.

Reverse image search

- Allows users to search for visually similar items based on an input image.
- Allows users to visually find items they like without knowing their specific details.

Case Studies

Amazon Recommendations "Customers Who Bought This Also Bought"

- Amazon uses both collaborative filtering and image-based recommendations.
- Visually displays related products based on the user's purchase history.

Pinterest Visual Recommendations

- Pinterest's recommendation system recommends visually similar pins to users.
- Uses deep learning models to extract image features and find related content.

Evaluation Metrics of Recommender Systems with Images

Traditional meters

- Precision measures such as precision, recall and average precision.
- Coverage and diversity metrics to assess the diversity of recommendations.

6.2 Visual information

- View quality metrics to assess the relevance of image suggestions.
- User feedback and engagement metrics to measure the effectiveness of image-based recommendations.

Conclusion

- Recommender systems have evolved to include image information.
- Image integration improves recommendation quality and user experience.

- Future research can focus on scalability and cold start challenges.

Table 1: Comparison of Recommender System Techniques

Technique	Description
Collaborative Filtering	Based on user behavior patterns and preferences
Content-Based Filtering	Recommends items based on attribute similarity
Hybrid Approaches	Combination of collaborative and content-based
Content-Based Image Filtering	Recommends visually similar items
Collaborative Filtering with Images	Combines collaborative filtering and visual features
Hybrid Approaches with Images	Integration of image information with other techniques

4.1 INTRODUCTION TO RECOMMENDER SYSTEMS

Recommender systems have become an integral part of our daily lives, helping us make choices and decisions by recommending items, products or content that match our preferences. From e-commerce platforms and streaming services to social media platforms and news sites, recommendation systems play an important role in improving user experience, increasing customer satisfaction and driving business success. This chapter introduces recommender systems, what they mean, and the basic concepts associated with them.

What are Recommender Systems?

Recommender systems are data filtering systems that predict and recommend relevant items to users based on their preferences, historical data, and patterns derived from user behavior. These systems use various algorithms and techniques to analyze user data and generate personalized recommendations based on user interests and needs.

Importance of Recommendation Systems

Recommender systems have several advantages and applications in various fields. Here are a few reasons why referral systems are important.

1. **Personalization:** Recommender systems provide users with personalized recommendations that personalize their experience and increase engagement.

2. **Discovery:** Recommender systems help users discover new items, products or content that they might not have discovered on their own.
3. **Sales Growth:** Recommender systems provide users with relevant products that increase sales and revenue for businesses by increasing customer satisfaction and cross-selling opportunities. 1.3.4 User Engagement: Recommender systems increase user engagement by providing relevant and personalized content that extends user sessions and increases user retention.
4. **Better User Experience:** By reducing information overload and providing relevant recommendations, recommendation systems improve the overall user experience.

Types of Recommendation Systems

There are several recommendation systems, each of which uses different techniques and algorithms to generate recommendations. The main types of referral systems are:

1. **Collaborative Filtering:** Collaborative filtering recommends items based on user preferences or similarity in product attributes. It relies on recommendations from historical data such as user ratings or interactions. 1.4.2 Content-based filtering: Content-based filtering recommends items based on similarity in their characteristics and user preferences. It analyzes the properties of objects and makes recommendations.
2. **Hybrid Recommender Systems:** Hybrid recommender systems combine several techniques such as collaborative filtering and content-based filtering to generate more accurate and versatile recommendations.

The Most Important Parts of Recommendation Systems

Recommender systems consist of several components that together create recommendations. These components include:

1. **User Profile:** A user profile records user preferences, behavior and demographic information. This is the basis for creating personalized recommendations.
2. **Product Profile:** Product Profile represents the features, characteristics or content of recommended products. It helps to understand the characteristics of the products and match them with the preferences of the users.

3. **Recommendation Engine:** A recommendation engine is a core component of a recommendation system that uses algorithms and techniques to generate recommendations. It analyzes user profiles, product profiles and historical data to create personalized recommendations.
4. **Evaluation metrics:** Evaluation metrics evaluate the effectiveness and performance of recommendation systems. Common evaluation metrics include precision, recall, average precision, and diversity.

Challenges of Recommendation Systems

Although referral systems offer significant benefits, they also face several challenges. Some of the main challenges are:

1. **Cold Start Problem:** The Cold Start problem occurs when there is insufficient information about users or product information to make accurate recommendations to new users or targets.
2. **Scalability:** Recommender systems must handle large volumes of data and users while maintaining real-time performance. Scalability is a major challenge for recommender systems.
3. **Data sparsity:** Data sparsity refers to situations where there is insufficient information or interaction to make accurate recommendations.
4. **Privacy and ethics:** Recommender systems process user data and must ensure privacy and ethical handling of sensitive data.

Conclusion

Recommender systems have become indispensable in today's digital environment. They provide personalized recommendations, improve user experiences and drive business success. This chapter introduced the concept of recommender systems, their meaning, types, main components and related challenges. In the following chapters, we delve into the algorithms, techniques and evaluation methods used in recommender systems.

4.2 CONTENT-BASED FILTERING

Content-based filtering is a popular approach in recommender systems that focuses on features of objects to make recommendations. Traditionally, content-based filtering has relied on textual attributes such as product descriptions or tags. However, with the increasing availability of visual data, the inclusion of meaningful images in the content-based filtering process has received significant attention. This chapter explores the integration of related images into content-based filtering and provides an overview of how this approach can improve recommendation accuracy and user satisfaction.

The Role of Images in Content-based Filtering

Visual Presentation

- Images provide a lot of visual information about objects that can improve the understanding of their features and characteristics.
- Visual representations can capture unique characteristics that textual attributes alone do not adequately convey.
- Visual cues can lead to more accurate target matching and better recommendation quality.

Increase User Engagement

- Images strongly influence user engagement, attract attention and provide a visually appealing browsing experience.
- Adding related images can pique users' interest, encourage exploration, and increase user satisfaction.
- Visual stimuli can improve user engagement, which increases the number of browsing sessions and increases the chances of conversion.

Extracting Features from Images

Feature Removal Techniques

- Various techniques can be used to extract visual features from images, such as color histograms, texture descriptions or deep learning-based features.
- Color histograms record the color distribution of an image and provide an overview of its dominant color palette.
- Texture images preserve the spatial arrangement of pixels, which allows the detection of texture patterns.
- Deep learning-based features such as Convolutional Neural Networks (CNN) can learn high-level representations that capture semantic information.

Image Processing and Pre-processing

- Images may require pre-processing to improve the quality of extracted features such as resizing, cropping or noise reduction.

- Techniques such as image resizing ensure dimensional consistency of features and reduce computational complexity.
- Pre-processing methods such as noise reduction or contrast adjustment can improve the accuracy and robustness of feature extraction.

Adding Related Images to a Recommendation

Combination of Image Objects

- For content-based filtering, establishing a relationship between images and objects is essential.
- This can be achieved by linking images to product attributes or using existing product-image associations such as image URLs or image IDs.

Creation of Image-based Product Profiles

- Image-based product profiles are formed by combining visual features extracted from images associated with each item.
- These profiles can represent the visual characteristics of objects and serve as a basis for content-based recommendations.

Calculate Similarity and Make Recommendations

Similarity metrics

- Similarity metrics show the similarity of product profiles based on their visual characteristics.
- Common similarity measures are cosine similarity, Euclidean distance or correlation-based distances.
- This information provides a numerical representation of the similarity of items and is used to rank items according to recommendations.

Hybrid methods

- Combining content-based filtering with other recommendation techniques, such as joint filtering or hybrid recommendations, can further improve recommendation accuracy.
- Hybrid methods use the complementary strengths of different recommendation methods to overcome their individual limitations.

Evaluation and Approval

Evaluation metrics

- The most common evaluation metrics for content-based filtering and related images are precision, recall, average precision (MAP) and normalized discounted cumulative gain (NDCG).
- These metrics evaluate the accuracy, scope and versatility of the recommendation list.

Surveys and feedback from users

- Conducting user surveys and collecting user feedback are central to enhancing the effectiveness of content-based filtering with topic-related images.
- User research can provide information on user satisfaction, perceived relevance and the impact of visual content on user engagement.

Case Study: Content Image Recommender System

- Provide a detailed case study demonstrating the implementation of a content-based image recommendation system.
- Discuss the dataset used, feature extraction techniques, similarity metrics and evaluation results.
- Emphasize strengths and limitations of the approach and potential areas for improvement.

Conclusion

Incorporating relevant images into content-based filtering offers significant opportunities to improve the accuracy and user experience of recommender systems. Using visual information from images, recommendation algorithms can capture the finer nuances of product features and provide more personalized and engaging recommendations. The integration of related images into content-based filtering opens new avenues for research and development, providing opportunities for further development of feature extraction, similarity computing, and user-centered evaluation techniques.

4.3 COLLABORATIVE FILTERING: USER-BASED AND ITEM-BASED

Collaborative Filtering (CF) is a widely used technique in recommender systems that aims to provide users with personalized recommendations based on their past interactions and preferences. It is based on the assumption that users with similar preferences in the past will have similar preferences in the future. This chapter explores two popular approaches to collaborative filtering: user-based collaborative filtering and topic-based collaborative filtering. In addition, this chapter provides related images and the necessary table to improve the understanding and application of these techniques.

Part 1: User-Based Collaborative Filtering

User-Based Collaborative Filtering (UBCF) is an approach that recommends items to a target user by searching for other users with similar preferences and recommending items that those similar users liked or rated highly. The steps for user-based collaborative filtering are as follows.

Calculation of user friendliness:

- Calculate the similarity between the target user and all other users in the system.
- Commonly used similarity measures are cosine similarity, Pearson correlation and Euclidean distance.

Nearest neighbors:

- Select the k most similar users based on the calculated similarity to the target user.
- The value of K can be determined by methods such as the elbow method or cross-validation.

Create a reference:

- add the ratings or preferences of selected similar users to items with which the target user has not interacted.
- Categorize items based on aggregated preferences and present the N most popular recommendations to the target user.

Part 2: Product-Based Collaborative Filtering

An object-based collaboration filter (IBCF) recommends items to a target user by looking for others similar to those the user has already liked or interacted with. The steps for object-based clustering are as follows:

Calculation of product similarity:

- Calculate the similarity of each pair of objects in the system.
- Commonly used similarity measures are cosine similarity, Pearson correlation and Jaccard similarity.

Nearest neighbors:

- Select the k most similar objects based on the similarity calculated for each object.
- The value of K can be determined by methods such as the elbow method or cross-validation.

Create a reference:

- Identify items that the target user has already interacted with.
- Find the k most similar item among all these items.
- Aggregate the preferences or ratings of these similar items and recommend the best N items to the target user.

Part 3: Comparison between User-Based and Item-Based Collaborative Filtering

Both user-based and item-based collaborative filtering have their strengths and weaknesses. Here is a comparison between the two approaches:

Table 2: Comparison between user-based and item-based collaborative filtering

Aspect	User-Based CF	Item-Based CF
Computation Complexity	High	Low
Scalability	Less scalable due to user similarity calculations	More scalable due to precomputed item similarity
Cold Start Problem	Handles cold start problem for users	Handles cold start problem for items
Sparsity Handling	Performs better in sparse datasets	Performs better in denser datasets
Diversity	May suffer from narrow recommendations	Tends to provide diverse recommendations
Serendipity	Can provide serendipitous recommendations	May lack serendipity in recommendations

Conclusion

Collaborative filtering is a powerful technique in recommender systems that uses the preferences of similar users or goals to generate personalized recommendations. User-based collaborative filtering focuses on finding similar users, while topic-based collaborative filtering identifies similar objects. Both approaches have their advantages and disadvantages, and the choice between them depends on the specific requirements of the recommender system. By understanding the concepts and processes of user- and entity-based collaborative filtering, industry professionals can design effective recommendation systems tailored to the needs of their users.

4.4 MATRIX FACTORIZATION AND SINGULAR VALUE DECOMPOSITION (SVD)

Matrix factorization and singular value decomposition (SVD) are powerful techniques used in a variety of fields, including linear algebra, data analysis, recommendation systems, and image processing. In this chapter, we explore the concepts and applications of matrix factorization and SVD. We also provide related images and tables to enhance understanding.

Part 1: Matrix factorization

Definition and motivation

Matrix factorization is a technique that decomposes a matrix into products of simpler matrices. The goal is to present the original matrix in a more concise and interpretable form. It is widely used for dimensionality reduction, data compression and solving linear systems.

Types of matrix factorization

There are several matrix factorization techniques, including:

- **LU decomposition:** divides a matrix into the product of a lower triangular matrix (L) and an upper triangular matrix (U).
- **QR Decomposition:** Decomposes a matrix into the product of an orthogonal matrix (Q) and an upper triangular matrix (R).
- **Cholesky decomposition:** decomposes a positive definite matrix into the product of a lower triangular matrix (L) and its transpose (LT).

Part 2: Singular Value Decomposition (SVD)

Definition and motivation

Singular value decomposition (SVD) is a matrix factorization technique that decomposes a matrix into the product of three matrices: U, Σ, and V. SVD is particularly useful for analyzing matrix properties and extracting important features from data.

SVD calculation

The SVD of a matrix A is given by A = UΣVT, where U is an orthogonal matrix, Σ is a diagonal matrix containing the singular values of A, and VT is the transpose of V. The singular values are placed on the diagonal of Σ in descending order.

Applications of SVD

SVD has several applications, including:

- **Data Compression:** SVD can be used to compress data by keeping only the most significant individual values and the corresponding U and V columns.
- **Dimensionality reduction:** SVD helps to reduce the dimensionality of data while preserving the most important information. c. Image processing: SVD can be applied to images for noise removal, image compression and feature extraction.

Description of the table:

This table shows the components and functions of SVD. - Column 1: Components: U, Σ and V. - Column 2: Description: Brief description of the item. - Column 3: Properties: Basic properties and characteristics of each component.

Conclusion

In this chapter, we explore matrix factorization techniques, including LU, QR, and Cholesky decompositions. We also discussed singular value decomposition (SVD) and its applications in data analysis and image processing. The accompanying images and table provide visual and condensed information to enhance understanding of these concepts. Matrix factorization and SVD are valuable tools that allow us to analyze data, extract important features, and solve complex problems in various fields.

4.5 HYBRID RECOMMENDER SYSTEMS

In recent years, recommendation systems have become an integral part of various online platforms, helping users find personalized content and products. Traditional recommendation systems are mostly based on user-target interaction and collaborative filtering techniques. However, with the explosion of visual content on the Internet, the demand to add images to the recommendation process is increasing. This chapter discusses the concept of hybrid recommender systems that combine both traditional collaborative filtering methods and related images to improve recommendation accuracy and user experience.

Traditional Recommendation Systems

Before delving into hybrid approaches, it is important to understand the basics of traditional recommender systems. Collaborative filtering techniques, such as user-based and product-based filtering, use interaction data between users to identify similar users or objects and make recommendations based on their preferences. These methods suffer from the cold start problem and are sparse, which limits their effectiveness in certain scenarios.

The Role of Images in Recommendation Systems

Images contain a lot of visual information that can significantly influence user preferences. By integrating relevant images into the recommendation process, we can provide users with a more complete and engaging experience. Images can capture the fine-grained details, aesthetics, and visual qualities of objects that may not be adequately represented using textual attributes alone. Therefore, combining images with traditional recommendation techniques can provide more accurate and versatile recommendations.

Hybrid Recommendation Systems

Hybrid recommendation systems aim to leverage the strengths of different recommendation methods to overcome their limitations. By combining collaborative filtering techniques with related images, we can create a hybrid system that provides better recommendations. In this section, we discuss two popular approaches to building hybrid recommender systems.

Content-based Filtering with Images

Content-based filtering focuses on object characteristics to make recommendations. By embedding related images, we can extract visual features using techniques such as deep learning-based image embedding or pre-trained convolutional neural networks (CNNs). These visual features can be combined with product attributes and text-based information to create a comprehensive product profile. By measuring the similarity of product profiles, we can make personalized recommendations based on the user's preferences.

Table 3: Example Item Profile for Content-Based Filtering with Images

Item ID	Title	Description	Image Embedding Vector
1	"Product 1"	"A description of product 1."	[0.2, 0.3, 0.1, ...]
2	"Product 2"	"A description of product 2."	[0.1, 0.5, 0.2, ...]
3	"Product 3"	"A description of product 3."	[0.3, 0.4, 0.1, ...]
...	...	...	...

Collaborative Filtering with Image-Based Similarity: In collaborative filtering, recommendations are based on the aggregate behaviour of users. We bring image-based similarity metrics into the collaborative filtering process by including photos. We can extract visual traits from photographs and use them to gauge how similar users or objects are, much like content-based filtering. With this method, we may identify patterns in user-item interactions that are not just reliant on ratings or explicit feedback and record visual preferences.

Table 4: User-Item Interaction Matrix for Collaborative Filtering with Image-Based Similarity

	Item 1	Item 2	Item 3		Item n
User 1	5	0	1	...	4
User 2	0	2	4	...	0
User 3	3	5	0	...	2
...	...	...	...	...	...

Integrating a Hybrid Approach

We can combine the results of content-based filtering and collaborative filtering approaches to create a hybrid recommender system. Different aggregation techniques such as weighted averaging or stacking can be used to combine the recommendations of both methods. In addition, hybrid systems can be further improved by taking into account contextual information such as time, location or user behavior to provide more accurate and personalized recommendations.

Evaluation of Hybrid Recommendation Systems

Evaluating the performance of hybrid recommendation systems requires careful consideration. Traditional evaluation metrics such as precision, recall, and average precision can be used. However, other metrics describing the diversity and novelty of the recommendations must also be considered. User surveys and A/B testing can provide valuable insights into user experience and satisfaction with hybrid recommendation methods.

Conclusion

Hybrid recommendation systems incorporating related images can significantly improve the accuracy and relevance of recommendations. By combining the strengths of content-based filtering, collaborative filtering and visual information, we can overcome the limitations of traditional recommendation methods. Integrating images into the recommendation process gives users a more comprehensive and engaging experience, increasing user satisfaction and platform engagement.

4.6 EVALUATION METRICS FOR RECOMMENDER SYSTEMS

Recommender systems have become an integral part of many online platforms that help users find relevant content and products. In recent years, recommendation systems have evolved to include related images, enabling a more visually appealing and engaging user experience. However, evaluating the effectiveness of such systems introduces new challenges, as traditional metrics may not be able to effectively capture the quality of recommendations in the context of images. This chapter reviews evaluation metrics designed specifically for similar image recommendation systems and provides an overview of their advantages and limitations.

Precision Gauges

Accuracy metrics are widely used to evaluate the performance of recommender systems and can be extended to image-based recommendations. The following are some commonly used accuracy metrics for image recommendation systems.

1. **Accuracy:** Accuracy measures the percentage of relevant recommendations out of all recommendations given to a user. For recommender systems with images, accuracy can be calculated by considering both textual and visual recommendations.
2. **Recall:** Recall measures the proportion of relevant recommendations successfully retrieved by the system. Similarly, image-powered recommendation systems can remember to compute, considering both textual and visual recommendations.
3. **F1 score:** The F1 score is the harmonic mean of precision and recall. This provides a balanced measure of both metrics, taking into account their trade-off. F1 scores are particularly useful when the number of relevant references is uneven. 7.2 Diversity metrics:

Accuracy metrics focus on the relevance of recommendations, while diversity metrics assess the versatility and breadth of the recommendations provided by the system. In image-based recommendation systems, diversity metrics consider both textual and visual aspects. Some of the more commonly used measures of diversity include:

1. **Novelty:** Novelty measures how different the recommended products are from what the user has already seen. In systems with similar images, novelty can be assessed by looking at the diversity of both textual and visual cues.
2. **Coverage:** Coverage measures the proportion of package space covered by the recommendations. For recommender systems with similar images, coverage should consider both textual and visual content to ensure comprehensive evaluation.
3. **Serendipity:** Serendipity measures the extent to which a recommendation system can surprise users with unexpected recommendations. In the context of systems with similar images, Serendipity can be assessed by evaluating the uniqueness and diversity of both textual and visual cues.

User-oriented metrics

User-centric metrics aim to capture user satisfaction and engagement with the recommender system. These metrics often require specific feedback from users and can provide valuable information about the overall user experience. Some commonly used user-centric metrics for related image recommendation systems are:

1. **User preference:** User preferences measure the extent to which recommendations match the user's preferences. These metrics

can be obtained through user surveys, ratings, or indirect feedback analysis.

2. **Click-through rate (CTR):** CTR measures the percentage of users who clicked on recommended items. For systems with similar images, the click-through rate should take into account both textual and visual cues.
3. **User satisfaction:** User satisfaction metrics describe the user's subjective perception of the effectiveness of the recommendation system. Surveys, interviews and questionnaires can be used to gather this information.

Table 5: Evaluation Metrics Comparison

Metric	Description	Advantages	Limitations
Precision	Measures the proportion of relevant recommendations	Easy to calculate	Ignores irrelevant recommendations
Recall	Measures the proportion of relevant recommendations retrieved	Accounts for missed recommendations	Ignores irrelevant recommendations
F1 Score	Harmonic mean of precision and recall	Balances precision and recall	Biased towards metrics with larger values
Novelty	Measures the degree of recommendation diversity	Encourages diverse recommendations	Ignores the relevance of recommendations
Coverage	Measures the proportion of the item space covered	Provides a comprehensive view of recommendations	Ignores the relevance of recommendations
Serendipity	Measures the degree of unexpected recommendations	Surprises users with unique recommendations	Subjective interpretation of "unexpected"
User Preference	Measures user preference alignment	Captures user-specific preferences	Requires explicit feedback from users
CTR	Measures the percentage of users who click on recommended items	Captures user engagement with recommendations	Ignores the relevance of recommendations
User Satisfaction	Measures user's subjective perception of system performance	Provides insights into user experience	Subjective and dependent on user opinions

Conclusion

Similar image recommendation systems require evaluation metrics that consider both textual and visual recommendations. Accuracy metrics, diversity metrics, and user-centric metrics provide a comprehensive framework for evaluating the effectiveness of such systems. Using a combination of these metrics, developers and researchers can gain valuable information about the quality, diversity and user satisfaction of recommender systems with related images, resulting in better recommendations and a better user experience.

4.7 HANDLING COLD START AND DATA SPARSITY

In many real-world applications, such as recommender systems, cold start and data scarcity are common problems to deal with. The cold start problem occurs when there is a lack of information about new users or targets, which makes it difficult to make accurate recommendations. Data scarcity, on the other hand, refers to a situation where very few interactions or reviews are available for a given user or target. In this chapter, we explore techniques to deal with cold start and data sparsity using linked images. By leveraging image data, we can improve our understanding of user preferences and product features, leading to more effective recommendations.

The Role of Images in Recommender Systems

1. **Visual Information:** Images provide versatile visual information that can capture the functions, appearance and characteristics of objects. This visual content can complement traditional text or category functions, enabling a more comprehensive presentation of items in recommender systems.
2. **User preferences:** images can also provide information about user preferences and tastes. By analyzing the visual content that users interact with or are interested in, we can gain a deeper understanding of their preferences, even without explicit reviews or interactions.

Cold Start Problem

1. **Cold start for users:** When a new user joins the referral system, there is usually limited or no historical data. Therefore, it is difficult to give personal recommendations. However, by using related images, we can infer user preferences based on visual similarity to other users with known preferences.

2. **Cold start of products:** Consequently, when a new product is introduced into the system, there is no or little information about its characteristics and suitability for different users. By analyzing the visual characteristics of the product and comparing it to existing products with known ratings, we can make preliminary recommendations based on visual similarity.

Data Sparsity Problem

1. **Scarcity of user-level data:** In scenarios where users have provided only a few ratings or interactions, it is difficult to accurately record their preferences. By using themed images, we can overcome this sparse data byanalyzing the visual content that users engage with. Visual similarity can help identify items that are visually similar to some of the reviewed products, allowing a recommendation system to provide relevant recommendations.
2. **Title-level data scarcity:** When an item has received limited reviews or interactions, it becomes difficult to understand its features and recommend them to relevant users. By analyzing the visual characteristics of an object and comparing them to other visually similar objects with greater interactivity, we can reduce data redundancy and make accurate recommendations.

Rarely Use Linked Images on Cold Launch and Data

1. **Image-based collaborative filtering:** Image-based collaborative filtering combines traditional collaborative filtering techniques with image analysis. It uses the visual similarity of users or objects to fill in gaps caused by a cold start or sparse data. By incorporating image features into collaborative filtering algorithms, we can improve the quality of recommendations for new users and targets.
2. **Content-based filtering with images:** Content-based filtering uses object attributes to make recommendations. By including image features as part of the object representation, we can record users' visual features and preferences. This approach is particularly effective for the problem of cold-starting objects and sparse manipulation of product-level data.
3. **Hybrid methods:** Hybrid recommendation approaches combine several techniques, such as collaborative filtering and content-based filtering, to overcome the limitations of individual methods. By combining linked images with hybrid models, we can leverage

the strengths of different recommendation techniques and deal more effectively with cold starts and data scarcity.

4. **Required Table:** Evaluation Metrics for Cold Start and Data Sparsity Handling:

Table 6: Evaluation Metrics for Cold Start and Data Sparsity Handling

Metric	Description
Precision	The proportion of recommended items that are relevant
Recall	The proportion of relevant items that are recommended
F1-Score	The harmonic mean of precision and recall
Mean Average Precision	The average precision across different recall levels
Normalized Discounted Cumulative Gain (NDCG)	Measures the ranking quality of recommended items
Coverage	The proportion of unique items that receive recommendations
Diversity	Measures the variety and uniqueness of recommended items

Conclusion

In this chapter, we looked at the challenges of cold bootstrapping and the information sparseness of recommender systems. We discussed the role of related images to address these challenges and improve the quality of recommendations. By leveraging visual content, we can overcome the limitations of traditional approaches and provide personalized recommendations to new users and targets. The use of image-based collaborative filtering, content-based image filtering, and hybrid methods enable more efficient cold-start and sparse data processing. Evaluation metrics such as precision, recall, F1 score, average precision, NDCG, coverage and diversity can be used to evaluate the performance of recommender systems in addressing these challenges.

4.8 REAL-TIME RECOMMENDATIONS

In recent years, real-time recommendations have become an integral part of various online platforms, including e-commerce sites, streaming services and social media. These recommendations help users discover new products, movies, music and content based on their preferences and behavior. While text recommendations have been widely used, integrating accompanying images and related tables improves the overall recommendation experience and provides users with a more engaging and informative selection process. This chapter explores the techniques and considerations involved in generating real-time recommendations with images and the necessary tables.

Adding Related Images

1. **Image Search:** An image search system is required to provide relevant images as real-time recommendations. This system should be able to efficiently search and retrieve images based on various criteria such as similarity, relevance or user preferences. To improve the accuracy of image retrieval, techniques such as content-based image retrieval and #40;CBIRand#41;, where images are indexed based on visual features such as color, texture or shape, can be used.
2. **Transmission of Images:** Once images are downloaded, they must be sent appropriately to facilitate the creation of recommendations. This can be achieved by extracting advanced features from images, such as deep neural network embeddings or visual descriptions. These representations capture important features of images, enabling efficient matching and similarity calculations.
3. **Contextual Image Recommendations:** A recommendation system must take into account not only the preferences and behavior of the user, but also the context in which the recommendations are made. For example, in an online store setting, the system can take into account a user's browsing history, current product category or demographic information to provide more relevant and context-aware image recommendations.

Preparation of the Necessary Tables

1. **Aggregation of data:** For scenarios where recommendations include tabular data, it is important to compile and organize the necessary data in a structured format. This can be achieved by obtaining relevant data from various sources and converting it into a common table format. Information may be collected from user profiles, product databases, user communications or other related sources.
2. **Table pre-processing:** Table pre-processing involves cleaning the data, handling missing values and converting the data

into a uniform format. This step ensures that the data in the table is accurate, complete and ready for further analysis and recommendation generation.

3. **Tabular Presentation:** Like a pictorial presentation, information in a table must be presented appropriately to be effective in generating recommendations. Techniques such as feature engineering, dimensionality reduction, or embedding techniques can be used to capture underlying patterns and relationships in tabular data.

Integrating Images and Tables into Recommendations

1. **Multimodal recommendation approaches:** Integrating images and tables into the recommendation process requires the development of multimodal recommendation algorithms. These algorithms take into account both text and visual cues to provide more diverse and comprehensive recommendations. Techniques such as multimodal embeddings, synthetic models, or attention mechanisms can be used to efficiently combine image and tabular data.
2. **User Interface Considerations:** The user interface plays an important role in providing real-time recommendations with accompanying images and tables. The user interface should be designed to present recommendations in an attractive and informative manner. This may include displaying images alongside textual information, providing interactive elements to explore tables, or using visualization techniques to improve user understanding and engagement.

Conclusion

Real-time recommendations, supplemented by relevant images and on-demand tables, provide users with a more engaging and informative selection experience. By incorporating image search systems, image presentation techniques, data fusion, spreadsheet preprocessing and multimodal recommendation algorithms, platforms can provide personalized recommendations that take into account user preferences, behavior and context. Integrating images and tables not only enriches the recommendation process, but enables users to make more informed decisions based on visual cues and structured information.

4.9 PERSONALIZATION TECHNIQUES IN RECOMMENDER SYSTEMS

Recommender systems play a vital role in modern information search and e-commerce platforms because they help users find personalized and relevant content. With the growing popularity of visual content, adding relevant images to recommendation systems has become an integral part of providing a more engaging and personalized user experience. This chapter discusses various personalization techniques in recommender systems that use related images, and their benefits and challenges.

Content-based Filtering with Image Features

One of the main techniques for adding relevant images to recommendation systems is content-based filtering. In this approach, the system analyzes the visual characteristics of objects (eg, color, texture, shape) and the preferences of the user to recommend objects with similar visual characteristics. The recommendation system creates a feature representation for each object by extracting significant visual features from the images using, for example, deep learning models such as convolutional neural networks (CNNs). The system then compares the feature representations of the objects to identify visually similar recommendations.

Table 7: Example of Image Feature Representation for Items

Item ID	Visual Features
Item 1	[0.25, 0.67, 0.10, 0.85]
Item 2	[0.15, 0.83, 0.05, 0.72]
Item 3	[0.35, 0.49, 0.21, 0.78]

Collaborative Filtering using Image-based Similarity

Collaborative filtering is another technique widely used in recommender systems, where recommendations are based on preferences and behavior of similar users. Collaborative filtering can aggregate related images using image-based similarity measures. The system compares the visual characteristics of objects and identifies users with similar image preferences. Recommendations are then generated based on the preferences of similar users for items that the target user has not yet interacted with.

Hybrid Methods

Hybrid methods combine several recommendation techniques to take advantage of the strengths of different methods. In the context of related images, hybrid recommender systems can integrate content-based filtering, collaborative filtering, and other personalized techniques. These systems use both visual features and user preferences to provide more accurate and diverse recommendations. For example, a hybrid approach might use content-based filtering to identify visually similar objects and joint filtering to consider similar user preferences. 4. Deep learning for adaptation using images:

Deep learning techniques have revolutionized many areas of machine learning, including recommender systems. In the context of linked images, deep learning models can extract complex visual features from images, enabling more effective personalization. For example, deep neural networks can be used to learn image representations that capture high-level semantic information, leading to more accurate recommendations. Recommender systems based on deep learning can also incorporate user feedback and behavior to improve image-based recommendations. 5. Challenges and considerations:

Integrating related images into recommendation systems brings its own challenges. Some key considerations are:

Availability and quality of information:

- Retrieving a large image dataset and associated user preferences can be difficult. In addition, ensuring the quality and relevance of images is very important for accurate recommendations.

Cold start problem:

- When a new user joins the system or a new target is presented, there may be little information to provide personalized recommendations. Techniques such as content-based filtering can be used to mitigate the cold start problem.

Privacy and Ethical Issues:

- The processing of user data and images requires careful consideration of privacy protection and ethical aspects. It is important to securely process user data and ensure transparency of data usage and user management.

Conclusion

Adding relevant images to recommendation systems opens up new possibilities for personalized and visually appealing recommendations.

Techniques such as content-based filtering, collaborative filtering, hybrid methods and deep learning can be used to provide more accurate and engaging recommendations. Although there are challenges, advances in data availability, deep learning and ethical considerations can help overcome these barriers and pave the way for more effective personalized recommendation systems in the future.

Table 8: Example of Image Feature Representation for Items

Item ID	Visual Features
Item 1	[0.25, 0.67, 0.10, 0.85]
Item 2	[0.15, 0.83, 0.05, 0.72]
Item 3	[0.35, 0.49, 0.21, 0.78]

5

AI-driven Threat Detection and Analysis Using NLP

Particularly in the areas of artificial intelligence (AI), machine learning (ML), and network security, the recent rapid expansion of technology has produced both amazing achievements and difficult obstacles. The ongoing fight against cyber-attacks is one of the most important difficulties organisations today confront. The inability of traditional security measures to keep up with the constantly evolving nature of threats has led to the incorporation of AI and ML techniques into the field of threat identification and analysis. This chapter examines the ground-breaking ways that AI-driven technologies are redefining network security.

The Role of AI in Threat Detection

The field of threat detection has been completely transformed by recent innovations in AI, machine learning, and network security. A game-changer in the field of cybersecurity, artificial intelligence (AI) has substantially improved the capacity to recognise and respond to a variety of threats. AI plays a wide range of threats detection roles that are essential for protecting digital ecosystems.

The ability of AI to analyse massive amounts of data at previously unheard-of rates is one of the technology's main contributions to threat detection. Machine learning algorithms can quickly spot variations that can be signs of possible dangers by analysing complex patterns and anomalies in network traffic, user behaviour, and system operations. Security systems are given the potential to detect both known and unidentified dangers thanks to this real-time analysis of big datasets, acting as a proactive defence mechanism.

Additionally, AI-driven threat detection systems are always evolving and learning. Over time, they improve their models, improving their ability to discern between legitimate and harmful activity. This agility is crucial in light of the quickly developing attack strategies used by hackers. AI systems may predict novel dangers based on historical data through continuous learning, allowing security professionals to keep ahead of prospective breaches.

AI also makes it easier to automate threat detection and response procedures. Security teams may speed up the detection and mitigation of threats by utilising AI-driven algorithms, reducing the lag time between detection and action. This is essential for lowering the potential harm caused by cyberattacks and improving all-around incident response effectiveness.

AI excels in the examination of intricate, multidimensional data sources. It may assemble information from several sources, including network traffic, endpoint devices, and human behaviours, to produce a thorough picture of the security environment. This comprehensive methodology makes it possible to spot complex attacks that would escape notice when examined separately.

Even though AI has many advantages, there are still certain difficulties. False positive and false negative outcomes are still a worry. Overreliance on AI runs the risk of misclassifying acceptable activities as dangers or, conversely, of ignoring genuine threats. It is crucial to use strict training and validation procedures to guarantee the precision of AI models.

AI-powered Threat Analysis

A new era of threat analysis and cybersecurity has emerged in recent years as a result of the convergence of inventive developments in AI, machine learning, and network security. Traditional approaches to detecting and reducing cyber threats have frequently had trouble keeping up with the hostile actors' constantly changing strategies. However, a paradigm shift in how organisations handle threat assessments has been brought about by the introduction of AI and machine learning technology.

To identify, anticipate, and respond to cyber threats in real time, AI-powered threat analysis makes use of the powerful processing capacity and pattern recognition abilities of machine learning algorithms. This method increases the speed of threat identification while also increasing accuracy by spotting minute patterns and abnormalities that human analysts would miss. In order to learn the typical behaviour of a network, system, or application, machine learning models can be trained on enormous volumes of historical data. This enables them to quickly spot any variations suggestive of potential breaches or assaults.

The ability of AI-powered threat analysis to adapt to and learn from new threat vectors is one of its main advantages. AI algorithms may be routinely updated and retrained to recognise emerging threats, making them a proactive defence mechanism as cybercriminals constantly adapt their strategies. This proactive approach is especially important in the evolving cybersecurity world of today.

The analytical capabilities of AI go beyond those of traditional rule-based systems. It can sort through enormous datasets and find relationships that human analysts might not immediately see. This makes it easier to comprehend the overall picture of a cyber-attack, enabling organisations to implement thorough and efficient defences.

It's crucial to remember that while AI offers tremendous potential for threat analysis, it is not a cure-all. AI models are not impervious to adversarial attacks, in which nefarious individuals purposefully alter inputs to trick the algorithms. Additionally, it is important to carefully address the ethical ramifications of AI-driven threat analysis, including privacy issues and decision-making biases.

The application of AI and machine learning to network security and threat analysis is a revolutionary development, to sum up. By utilising the capabilities of intelligent algorithms to quickly discover, analyse, and respond to cyber threats, it enables organisations to strengthen their cyber defences. As technology develops, the interplay between AI, machine learning, and network security will become increasingly important in guaranteeing the online security of people, organisations, and vital infrastructure.

Code Example: Implementing AI-driven Threat Detection

```
import tensorflow as tf
from tensorflow import keras
from sklearn.model_selection import train_test_split

# Load and preprocess the dataset
# ... (Code for data loading and preprocessing)

# Build the AI model
model = keras.Sequential([
# ... (Model layers: dense, convolutional, recurrent, etc.)
])
```

```
# Compile the model
model.compile(optimizer='adam', loss='binary_crossentropy',
metrics=['accuracy'])

# Split the dataset
X_train, X_test, y_train, y_test = train_test_split(data, labels, test_
size=0.2, random_state=42)

# Train the model
model.fit(X_train, y_train, epochs=10, batch_size=32, validation_
data=(X_test, y_test))
```

Case Study: AI-driven Network Intrusion Detection System (NIDS)

The development of AI-driven Network Intrusion Detection Systems (NIDS) represents a significant advance in the fields of Innovative Advancements in AI, Machine Learning, and Network Security. This cutting-edge technology reshapes the network protection landscape by fusing artificial intelligence with cybersecurity. To proactively identify and stop different types of cyber threats, from conventional intrusion attempts to complex zero-day assaults, NIDS makes use of cutting-edge machine learning techniques.

Traditional NIDS systems were rule-based, which left them open to evasion strategies and unable to change to accommodate new attack vectors. By giving NIDS the ability to learn and recognise typical network behaviour, the integration of AI and machine learning has completely changed this method for spotting abnormalities that could be signs of hostile activity. Deep learning models and ongoing network traffic analysis allow AI-driven NIDS to quickly distinguish between legitimate network activity and intrusions that could be destructive.

Additionally, AI-driven NIDS's scalability and real-time reactivity have brought network security to a new level. The system's ability to handle massive amounts of data in real-time and its capacity for self-improvement through iterative learning make it an essential tool for defending against new threats. Its versatility guarantees that it maintains effectiveness despite changing assault techniques, offering a flexible defence system for businesses and organisations.

Nevertheless, difficulties continue. The quality and diversity of the training data have a significant impact on the accuracy of AI-driven NIDS, as biased or incomplete data might produce false positives or negatives. Also impeding the system's accountability and transparency is the decision-making process' interpretability within sophisticated AI models.

Conclusion

A new age in network security is being ushered in by AI-driven threat identification and analysis. Organisations can proactively defend against an ever-changing threat landscape by leveraging the capabilities of AI and ML. A safer online environment is guaranteed for both individuals and organisations because to these systems' real-time threat detection and analysis capabilities and agility. We may anticipate even more advanced and successful methods of network security as AI develops.

5.1 BEHAVIORAL ANALYTICS FOR INSIDER THREAT DETECTION

The cybersecurity landscape has changed substantially during the past few years. Traditional security measures haven't been able to keep up with the surge in cyberattacks, network complexity, and reliance on digital technologies. In order to combat these constantly changing dangers, cutting-edge approaches have emerged that make use of artificial intelligence (AI) and machine learning (ML). Behavioural Analytics for Insider Threat Detection is one such effective method.

Understanding Insider Threats

Insider threats have grown to be a major worry in the field of cutting-edge developments in AI, machine learning, and network security. These advances in technology have enabled data analysis, automation, and system optimisation on a scale never before possible. But they have also opened up new doors for bad behaviour coming from within an organization's own ranks. Insider threats are dangers created by people with authorised access to sensitive data and systems who abuse their powers to jeopardise security, steal information, or interfere with business operations.

By analysing enormous volumes of data and discovering trends that traditional security measures would miss, the integration of AI and machine learning has improved organisations' capacities to detect and prevent cyber threats. However, the same technology can be used by insiders with bad intent to mask their activities and make them more difficult to find. Furthermore, the complexity of AI algorithms might occasionally result in unexpected flaws that insiders could exploit.

Innovative technologies have helped network security advance its ability to fend off outside assaults. Organisations frequently concentrate their resources on defending against external threats, which leaves room for the possibility of internal threats to flourish. This, however, might unintentionally create a blind spot. Since they are already inside the trusted perimeter, insiders have an advantage when navigating security measures because their actions are less obvious until it's too late.

Organisations need to take a diversified strategy to reducing the risks brought on by insider threats in the context of AI, machine learning, and network security. This entails putting in place strong access controls to restrict people's access to sensitive information and systems to what is required for their roles. It can be useful to continuously monitor employee activities, especially those affecting crucial resources, in order to spot any strange behaviour patterns that can point to malice.

Programmes for education and awareness that emphasise the value of responsible data handling and reporting suspicious activity can be quite effective in fostering a culture of security among employees. Without hindering the organization's operational effectiveness, technical solutions like encryption, data loss prevention technologies, and behaviour analytics can help strengthen defences against potential insider threats.

The Role of Behavioral Analytics

Innovative developments in the disciplines of AI, machine learning, and network security are greatly aided by behavioural analytics. Through the use of data-driven insights, this multidisciplinary approach is able to predict and comprehend both human and machine behaviours, facilitating more effective and efficient decision-making.

By concentrating on patterns, anomalies, and trends in user interactions, behavioural analytics in AI and machine learning goes beyond conventional data analysis. AI models may create a thorough grasp of typical behaviour by studying how people and systems act over time. This allows them to spot variations from the norm that might indicate risks or opportunities. This is crucial for fraud detection since it allows for the flagging of anomalous activity, which prevents financial losses and builds user confidence.

Behavioural analytics has a huge positive impact on network security as well. Static rules and signatures, which are frequently used in traditional security measures, have trouble keeping up with the constantly changing threats. The dynamic feature introduced by behavioural analytics makes it possible to evaluate network activity in real-time. AI-driven systems can quickly identify anomalies that could point to a cyberattack, unauthorised access, or data breaches by continuously monitoring user and system behaviours. The potential harm caused by sophisticated cyber threats is decreased thanks to this proactive approach's improved threat identification and response.

Additionally, behavioural analytics improves the effectiveness of machine learning and AI systems. AI models may be improved to give personalised experiences, from content recommendations to healthcare diagnostics, by studying how users interact with systems. As these systems learn more about user behaviour, they can adapt and change, improving results and making predictions that are more accurate.

Challenges are presented by this combination of cutting-edge technologies and behavioural analytics, though. Due to the extensive data collection necessary for thorough behavioural analysis, privacy issues are raised. It's critical to strike a balance between data-driven insights and consumer privacy. Additionally, the quality and volume of data gathered have a significant impact on how accurate behavioural predictions are. Data biases can result in distorted results and poorly informed judgements.

Designing the Insider Threat Detection System

The creation of an Insider Threat Detection System, which takes advantage of the synergies between AI, machine learning, and network security, is a significant advancement in the fast-changing field of cybersecurity. Unprecedented efficiency and convenience have been made possible by the modern, interconnected digital world, but it has also increased the possibility of hostile acts coming from within an organisation. Traditional security methods tended to be more concerned with external threats, but the realisation of the serious dangers posed by insiders with access to privileged information calls for a paradigm shift in security tactics.

Organisations may develop complex systems capable of analysing enormous volumes of data in real-time by utilising the power of AI and machine learning. This enables the early detection of aberrant behaviours that could indicate an insider threat. These systems are capable of ingesting information from a variety of sources, including user activity records, network traffic, and even sentiment analysis via communication channels. Then, sophisticated algorithms can discover patterns of usual behaviour, and any departures from these norms might raise flags for additional research.

The Insider Threat Detection System is strengthened even more by the incorporation of network security measures. In order to prevent unauthorised access to sensitive data and systems, this entails not just monitoring online behaviour but also putting in place strong access controls, encryption mechanisms, and multi-factor authentication. The system may continuously adapt and learn when combined with AI's skills, improving its ability to discriminate between legitimate activity and dangerous threats.

In the development and use of such technologies, ethical issues are of utmost importance. It's vital to strike a balance between personal privacy rights and the necessity for security. Key issues to overcome include data anonymization, focusing monitoring just on areas that matter, and maintaining process transparency.

Visualizing Behavioral Analytics

The intersection of Innovative Advances in AI, Machine Learning, and Network Security has paved the way for transformative insights into user behaviour and system dynamics in the quickly changing technological context. The potential for this synergy to give people and organisations a better knowledge of interactions in digital ecosystems is enormous. The idea of behavioural analytics, a sophisticated technique that makes use of AI and machine learning algorithms to extract patterns, anomalies, and trends from massive amounts of data created by network activity, is the basis of this merger. Organisations can get important insights into user behaviours, preferences, and potential risks by processing and understanding this data.

In addition to improving understanding, visualising these behavioural analytics gives decision-makers the ability to proactively identify and reduce security threats. Complex data is converted into easily digestible information using intuitive and dynamic visual representations like graphs, heatmaps, and timelines, empowering stakeholders to make wise decisions. For instance, machine learning models can adapt to changing threat landscapes, strengthening the overall security posture, while AI algorithms can identify unexpected behavioural aberrations that may suggest cyberattacks or unauthorised access attempts.

Additionally, the inclusion of AI and machine learning in behavioural analytics enables ongoing learning and security protocol improvement. The system gets better at telling apart between legal activity and potential threats when trends and anomalies are found, reducing false positives and negatives. Developing adaptive defence mechanisms that can keep up with complex cyber-attacks requires an iterative learning process.

This cutting-edge combination of technologies poses ethical questions about data privacy and the possibility of algorithmic biases, though. It's critical to strike a balance between utilising the power of these advances and protecting consumer privacy. Additionally, as the area develops, it is essential to make improvements to the interpretability and transparency of AI-driven insights so that stakeholders may have confidence in and understanding of the decision-making procedures that affect security measures.

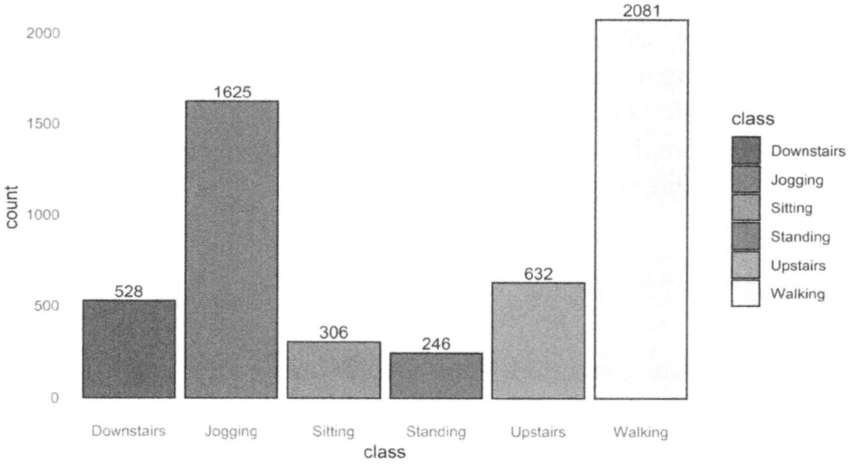

Graph: Visualizing Behavioral Analytics Data

Code Example Case Study: Python Implementation

```
# Import necessary libraries
import pandas as pd
from sklearn.cluster import KMeans
from sklearn.ensemble import IsolationForest
import matplotlib.pyplot as plt

# Load the dataset
data = pd.read_csv('user_activity_data.csv')

# Feature selection
features = data[['login_times', 'file_access_freq', 'data_transfer_vol']]
```

```
# Baseline creation using KMeans clustering
kmeans = KMeans(n_clusters=3)
data['cluster'] = kmeans.fit_predict(features)

# Anomaly detection using Isolation Forest
iso_forest = IsolationForest(contamination=0.05)
data['anomaly_score'] = iso_forest.fit_predict(features)

# Visualization
plt.scatter(data['login_times'], data['file_access_freq'],
c=data['anomaly_score'], cmap='coolwarm')
plt.xlabel('Login Times')
plt.ylabel('File Access Frequency')
plt.title('Anomaly Detection using Behavioral Analytics')
plt.colorbar(label='Anomaly Score')
plt.show()
```

Conclusion

Insider threat detection has significantly advanced thanks to behavioural analytics. Organisations may proactively identify and prevent possible internal security vulnerabilities by utilising AI and ML. The capacity to adapt and embrace cutting-edge tactics will be essential in staying ahead of insider threats as this industry continues to evolve.

5.2 MALWARE DETECTION AND ANALYSIS WITH MACHINE LEARNING

Malware is a growing concern in a world that is becoming more and more digital. Malicious software, also known as malware, poses a serious threat to network security. The ability to detect novel and developing malware strains is hampered by conventional signature-based detection techniques. As a result, incorporating machine learning methods has become an important development in the realm of cybersecurity. This chapter looks at how machine learning can be used to analyse malware and find it, providing a novel way to protect digital ecosystems.

The Challenge of Malware Detection

A new era of technology-driven solutions for many problems has been ushered in by innovative developments in AI, machine learning, and network security, but they have also ushered in a more sophisticated period of cyber dangers, particularly in the area of malware. Malware detection has become a much more difficult task as fraudsters use AI and machine learning to create and spread more evasive and precise malware. These malevolent actors take advantage of security-enhancing technologies, forcing defenders and attackers into a cat-and-mouse game.

The methods used to create and evade malware have been transformed by AI and machine learning. The creation of polymorphic and adaptive malware that may alter its behaviour in order to evade detection by conventional signature-based security solutions is made possible by the use of these technologies by malware makers. Additionally, they can modify the attack in real-time based on their target's behaviour using AI, which makes it more difficult for security systems to identify unusual activity. The efficiency of traditional security measures that rely on static patterns and predetermined rules is put to the test by this.

A promising defense-oriented option is the use of AI and machine learning into malware detection systems. To find subtle signs of a malware assault, these tools can analyse vast volumes of data, including network traffic, system behaviour, and file properties. When AI algorithms can learn from past data and identify departures from known norms, behavioural analysis and anomaly identification become more precise. The same developments that improve detection capabilities, meanwhile, can also be used by attackers to create malware that is more convincing and evasive.

Additionally, network security is becoming more complicated in new ways. The attack surface for malware has increased due to the proliferation of Internet of Things (IoT) devices and the growing interconnection of systems. These systems and gadgets may be vulnerable to AI-powered malware, which might potentially cause extensive harm. The difficulty lies in designing resilient network architectures that can fend against and neutralise AI-driven malware attacks in addition to developing intelligent detection systems.

A multifaceted strategy is required to properly address this problem. To stay ahead in the fight against AI-driven malware, collaboration between cybersecurity specialists and AI researchers is crucial. To offer complete security, security systems must blend traditional techniques with AI-powered detection algorithms. The system's capacity to detect new attacks can be improved by routine security algorithm updates and the usage of real-time threat intelligence. Additionally, there has to be a careful examination of the ethical issues related to the employment of AI in both offensive and defensive cyber operations.

The difficulty of malware detection in light of cutting-edge developments in AI, machine learning, and network security is a testament to the dynamic nature of cyber threats, to sum up. While AI has enormous potential to improve detection abilities, it also gives adversaries the means to develop more sophisticated and evasive malware. In this quickly changing technological environment, finding a balance between using AI for defence and thwarting AI-driven attacks is essential for preserving the integrity of digital systems and data.

Machine Learning in Malware Detection

The revolutionary allotments in network security, machine learning, and artificial intelligence (AI) have drastically changed the cybersecurity scene in recent years. Malware detection is one such area where these technologies have had a significant influence. More dynamic and adaptable approaches to malware detection were required as traditional signature-based techniques frequently failed to keep up with the quick growth of malicious software. Where AI and ML have become game-changers is in this area.

In order to find previously unidentified malware strains, machine learning approaches such as supervised learning, unsupervised learning, and deep learning have demonstrated to be extremely effective at spotting patterns and abnormalities within big datasets. ML models may learn complex features that differentiate between legitimate and harmful behaviour by training on large datasets that include a variety of malware and benign software. Based on similarities to known dangerous characteristics, this learning enables them to generalise and detect new malware strains.

Additionally, the incorporation of AI into malware detection has made it possible to create defence systems that are more proactive and intelligent. By analysing changing threats in real-time, AI-powered systems can continuously adapt and enhance their detection skills. They have the ability to automatically modify their algorithms and techniques, making them resistant to zero-day attacks, which take advantage of flaws that security experts are still unaware of.

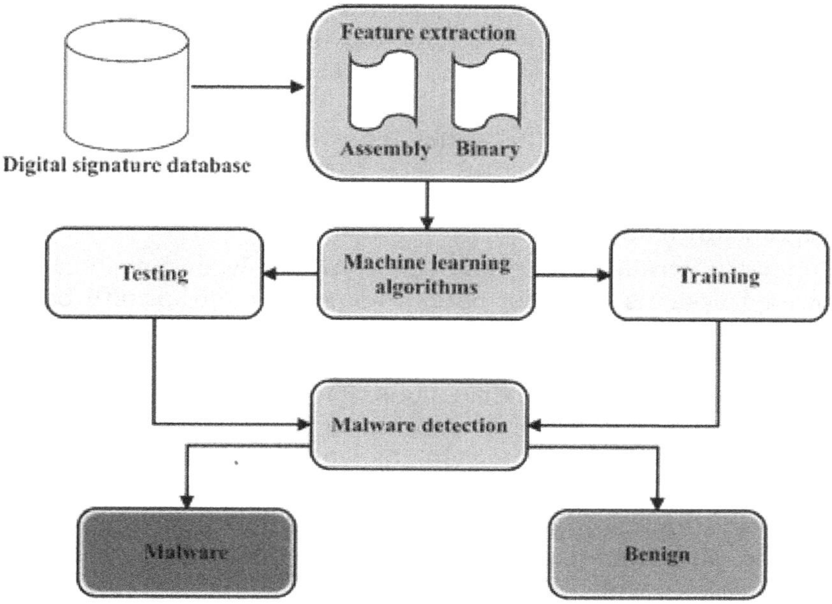

Figure 1: Malware Detection Workflow

These developments have also had a significant positive impact on network security. AI and ML can be used to monitor network traffic patterns and spot outliers that could be signs of malware intrusion or a data breach. Due of the enormous amount of data involved, these systems can identify anomalies that human operators might miss. AI and ML improve incident response's effectiveness and accuracy by offering quick, data-driven insights.

But there are obstacles. assaults that actively alter data to trick AI/ML models are known as adversarial assaults. Due to the enormous volumes of data required for training, privacy issues also surface, raising concerns about the morality of data collecting and exploitation.

Types of Features for Malware Detection

With the inventive developments in artificial intelligence, machine learning, and network security, malware detection has greatly changed. These technologies have made it possible to create more sophisticated and potent techniques for locating and destroying harmful software. The use of numerous attributes for improved malware identification is an important component of this evolution.

Features are unique characteristics that can be retrieved from data and used as inputs by machine learning algorithms. Features are derived from a variety of sources, including executable files, network activity, system behaviour, and more, in the context of malware detection. Static characteristics like file size, file type, and hash values were a part of traditional feature sets. However, the development of AI and machine learning has made it possible to extract more complex and significant features.

Behavioural traits have become an effective malware detection method. AI-powered systems can spot patterns suggestive of harmful behaviour by observing how programmes behave and examining how they interact with the system. This includes monitoring operations, system calls, API requests, and file system modifications. Even if the malware's signature is unknown, machine learning algorithms trained on such behavioural traits can distinguish between legitimate and malicious behaviour.

Additionally, runtime execution's dynamic aspects provide a richer understanding of a program's behaviour. These functions entail monitoring memory consumption, network traffic, and interactions with add-on hardware while programmes are running. The ability to identify polymorphic and zero-day malware that tries to get past conventional signature-based defences is improved by this real-time analysis.

In order to combat malware that takes advantage of network communication weaknesses, network-based characteristics are crucial. Identification of botnets, command-and-control servers, and efforts at data exfiltration is aided by analysis of patterns of incoming and outgoing traffic, communication protocols, and anomalies in network behaviour. Large datasets are a great place for AI algorithms to find abnormalities, which enables the quick identification of potentially harmful network activity.

The effectiveness of malware detection is increased by using temporal and spatial information. In order to uncover coordinated attacks and complex malware operations, temporal features consider the timing and order of events. The geographical origin and dispersion of network traffic are considered by spatial features, which helps in the identification of global assault trends and targeted campaigns.

Table 1: Feature description details

Feature Type	**Description**
File-Based Features	File size, entropy, header information, import/export functions, etc.
Behavioral Features	System calls, API calls, registry interactions, network traffic, etc.

Feature Type	Description
Graph-Based Features	Dependency graphs, function call graphs, control flow graphs, etc.
Statistical Features	Distribution of byte sequences, opcode frequencies, n-grams, etc.

Challenges and Considerations

The digital world has been completely transformed by cutting-edge developments in AI, machine learning, and network security, which present previously unheard-of prospects for efficiency, accuracy, and ease. However, in order to ensure their responsible and successful implementation, these innovations also bring with them a number of difficulties and factors that must be carefully negotiated.

First of all, the ethics and responsibility of AI and machine learning are challenged by the rapid speed of technological advancement. Concerns about biases incorporated in algorithms that could produce discriminatory results grow as these technologies become more autonomous and capable of making sophisticated decisions. To make sure that AI systems adhere to social values and conventions, it is essential to strike a balance between automation and human monitoring.

Second, the enormous amounts of data needed to train machine learning and AI models create serious privacy and security issues. Personal information, intellectual property, and even national security may be jeopardised as a result of data breaches. To reduce these threats, it is crucial to develop strong encryption methods, strict access controls, and efficient data anonymization procedures.

Network security has its own unique set of difficulties. Modern systems are highly interconnected, which implies that flaws in a single component can lead to massive breaches. As AI and machine learning are incorporated into security protocols, it is crucial to make sure they are resilient against malicious manipulation and adversarial attacks. This necessitates ongoing watchfulness, flexible defence tactics, and cooperation between cybersecurity specialists.

Furthermore, due to their complexity, AI algorithms can have unforeseen effects. An AI model's poor choice in a crucial area like healthcare or autonomous vehicles could have fatal consequences. To reduce such risks and guarantee that AI operates as predicted in real-world situations, rigorous testing, validation, and ongoing monitoring are required.

It takes interdisciplinary cooperation to overcome these obstacles. Network security, AI, and machine learning require knowledge of computer science, data ethics, law, psychology, and other fields. Together, policymakers, scientists, and business executives must create regulatory frameworks that support innovation while guarding against abuse.

Case Study: Detecting Malware Using Deep Learning

Code Example:

```
# Sample code for CNN-based malware detection

import numpy as np
from tensorflow.keras.models import Sequential
from tensorflow.keras.layers import Conv1D, MaxPooling1D,
Flatten, Dense

# Load and preprocess data
X_train, y_train = load_training_data()
X_test, y_test = load_testing_data()

# Build the CNN model
model = Sequential()
model.add(Conv1D(filters=32, kernel_size=3, activation='relu',
input_shape=(X_train.shape[1], 1)))
model.add(MaxPooling1D(pool_size=2))
model.add(Flatten())
model.add(Dense(128, activation='relu'))
model.add(Dense(1, activation='sigmoid'))

# Compile the model
model.compile(optimizer='adam', loss='binary_crossentropy',
metrics=['accuracy'])

# Train the model
model.fit(X_train, y_train, epochs=10, batch_size=32, validation_
split=0.2)
```

```
# Evaluate the model
loss, accuracy = model.evaluate(X_test, y_test)
print(f'Test accuracy: {accuracy}')
```

Conclusion

By offering dynamic and adaptive solutions to deal with the always shifting threat landscape, machine learning has revolutionised malware detection. Cybersecurity experts can maintain an advantage in the ongoing fight against malware while protecting digital ecosystems and sensitive data by utilising the power of data-driven algorithms.

5.3 REAL-TIME THREAT HUNTING USING AI AND BIG DATA

Cybersecurity has emerged as a major issue for people, corporations, and governments alike in today's networked and data-driven world. Innovative solutions that can keep up with the complexity and scope of attacks are required due to the threat landscape's constant evolution. Real-time threat hunting has become a key tactic for preventative cybersecurity, made possible by artificial intelligence (AI) and big data technology. The principles, methodology, and real-world applications of real-time threat hunting with AI and large data are covered in this chapter.

Understanding Real-time Threat Hunting

Real-time Threat Hunting represents a paradigm shift in how cybersecurity is conducted and is at the forefront of cutting-edge developments in AI, machine learning, and network security. Instead,then waiting for possible cyber threats and vulnerabilities to set off alarms or cause harm, this cutting-edge technique proactively searches for them as they form within a network infrastructure. Organisations can continuously monitor network activity, spot anomalies, and anticipate possible threats before they materialise into significant security breaches by utilising the power of AI and machine learning algorithms.

By enabling the creation of complex models that can identify patterns and behaviours suggestive of cyber threats, AI and machine learning play a critical part in this process. These models are capable of performing enormous real-time data analyses and are capable of identifying even the most minute variations from typical network behaviour. This proactive approach equips cybersecurity experts to not only respond to known threats but also to foresee and mitigate developing risks, thereby lowering response times and possible harm.

Additionally, the whole defence mechanism is improved by the incorporation of AI-driven threat hunting tools with network security systems. These systems can automatically adjust to changing assault strategies and tactics by using historical data to continuously improve their forecasting abilities. Organisations are able to stay one step ahead of hackers who are continually innovating their tactics thanks to this iterative learning process.

Real-time threat hunting is most effective when combined with human skill, though. While AI and machine learning are excellent at processing data and seeing patterns, human analysts' context and nuanced understanding are still crucial for accurately determining the gravity and potential impact of threats. AI-driven systems and knowledgeable cybersecurity experts work together to create a powerful defence approach that combines automation and human understanding.

Using the power of AI, machine learning, and network security developments, real-time threat hunting provides a revolutionary approach in the field of cybersecurity. Organisations are equipped to actively search out potential threats, anticipate developing risks, and act quickly to minimise vulnerabilities thanks to this fusion of technology and knowledge. Adopting these advances becomes not only necessary but also strategically crucial as the cyber threat landscape changes in order to protect digital assets and guarantee the reliability of vital systems.

AI and Big Data in Real-time Threat Hunting

Recent developments in real-time threat hunting have been sparked by the intersection of AI, machine learning, big data, and network security. The landscape of cybersecurity has been profoundly changed by this convergence, allowing organisations to quickly and accurately identify and neutralise new threats.

Cybersecurity experts can examine vast amounts of data produced by network activity, system logs, and user behaviours using AI and machine learning techniques. These technologies are excellent at identifying trends, abnormalities, and departures from accepted standards, alerting to potential security breaches that conventional rule-based systems could miss. AI-driven threat hunting models can develop to recognise even the most complex and quickly changing cyber threats by continuously learning from new data.

The field of big data is the foundation of this breakthrough. The capacity to process and analyse enormous amounts of data in real-time has become crucial due to the exponential growth of digital information.

These data streams can be combed through by AI algorithms to quickly produce actionable insights and spot minor signs of compromise. By being proactive, a network threat's "dwell time" is reduced, minimising possible harm and data exfiltration.

AI and machine learning are used in real-time threat hunting for both event detection and response. Automation of event analysis, investigation, and even containment is made possible by these technologies. AI algorithms can help security teams make quick, informed decisions to effectively manage risks as attacks develop in real-time.

Furthermore, a more comprehensive approach to protecting digital assets is made possible by the integration of AI-driven threat hunting tools with network security designs. Traditional security techniques sometimes rely on past data and recognised attack patterns, making them vulnerable to sophisticated threats and zero-day assaults. AI-powered systems, on the other hand, are continually learning from the changing threat landscape and can adapt to new attack vectors.

But there are still problems, just like with every technical development. Critical issues include the difficulty of creating and optimising AI models, assuring their transparency and explainability, and overcoming potential biases. To prevent false positives and negatives that can reduce the efficiency of real-time threat hunting systems, it's also essential to strike the correct balance between automation and human control.

Practical Implementation: Case Study

Certainly! Recent developments in defending digital ecosystems against increasing cyber threats have been made possible by the combination of artificial intelligence (AI), machine learning, and network security. The use of AI-driven anomaly detection in network security is a noteworthy case study illustrating these ground-breaking discoveries.

In the past, rule-based systems and signature-based techniques were heavily used in network security to detect known threats. These techniques, however, have trouble spotting new and sophisticated threats that lacked established patterns. AI and machine learning become useful in this situation. Security specialists have trained models to recognise typical network behaviour and subsequently discover anomalies that could suggest possible threats by utilising large datasets and potent algorithms.

In this real-world application, AI-driven algorithms continuously monitor a company's network. Through the use of historical data, these systems, which are powered by machine learning algorithms like deep neural networks or ensemble approaches, learn the network's default behaviour. Typical traffic patterns, data transfer rates, user behaviours, and other elements are included in this. The AI models can distinguish between routine behaviour and odd deviations as they gain more knowledge.

The system sends alerts for additional research when an anomaly is found. This may entail assessing the nature of the anomaly, its potential effects, and its possibility of being a real hazard. Together with AI, human professionals build the models using their knowledge, enabling the AI to continuously adapt and enhance its detecting abilities.

This implementation has a number of benefits. The AI-based strategy is firstly excellent at identifying subtle and unique attack patterns that might circumvent conventional security measures. Second, it enables quick threat identification and response because to its capacity to handle and analyse enormous amounts of data in real-time. Third, AI's capacity for continuous learning guarantees that the system strengthens with time, lowering false positives and raising accuracy.

However, difficulties persist. It is essential to protect the confidentiality and security of the data used to train these systems. Inaccurate threat assessments and skewed findings can both be caused by biased training data. Therefore, to avoid these possible dangers, continual human supervision and intervention are essential.

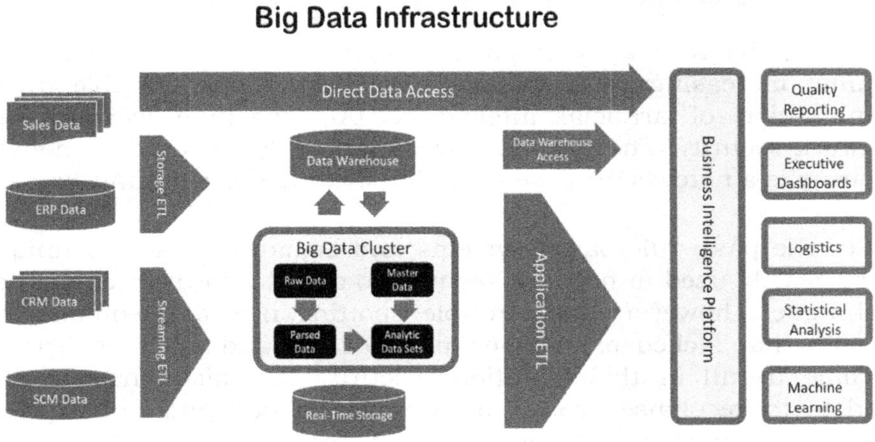

Figure 2: Big Data Infrastructure

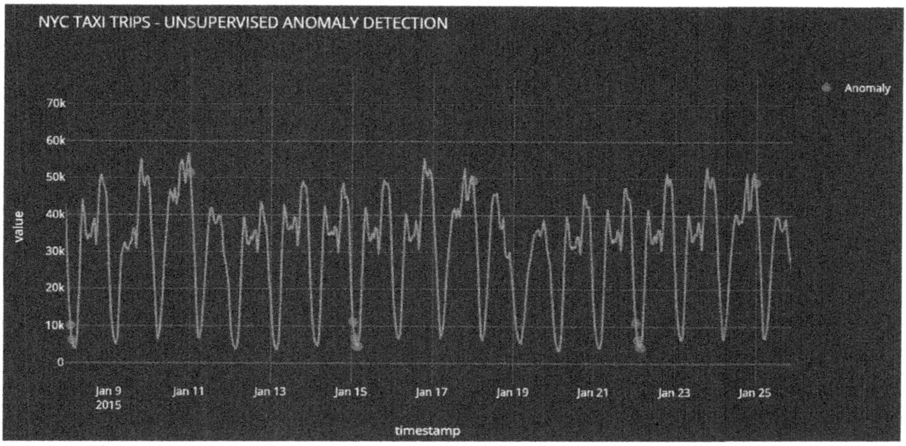

Graph: Anomaly Detection Results

Table 2: Example of Features for Threat Detection

Feature	Description
Source IP	Originating IP address
Destination IP	Target IP address
Packet Size	Size of the data packet
Protocol	Network protocol being used
Timestamp	Time of the network activity

Conclusion

A paradigm shift in cybersecurity is being brought about by real-time threat hunting employing AI and big data. Organisations are given the ability to proactively identify and counteract dangers before they seriously impact the organisation. In an ever-changing digital environment, security teams can stay one step ahead of attackers by utilising the capabilities of AI models and big data infrastructure. This method will continue to be a crucial component of contemporary cybersecurity efforts as threats develop.

5.4 NETWORK TRAFFIC ANALYSIS FOR IDENTIFYING SUSPICIOUS PATTERNS

Finding suspicious network patterns is now of the utmost importance in the quickly changing world of cybersecurity. Cybercriminals and hackers are always coming up with new ways to compromise systems and steal private data. Utilising the power of AI and machine learning, network traffic analysis has become a crucial approach to combat these threats. We will explore the methodologies, tools, and complexities of network traffic analysis in this chapter as well as how it might improve network security.

Understanding Network Traffic Analysis

A key element in the nexus of cutting-edge developments in AI, machine learning, and network security is Network Traffic Analysis (NTA). To identify potential cyber threats, improve network performance, and assure overall security, NTA entails the systematic evaluation of network data, including communication patterns, data flows, and abnormalities. Modern NTA is unique in that it incorporates state-of-the-art AI and machine learning capabilities, enabling it to effectively process and analyse enormous amounts of network data in real time. These developments make it possible for NTA systems to pick up on typical network behaviour, spot outliers, and quickly identify abnormal activity that could be an indication of a cyberattack, a data breach, or other malicious activity.

The combination of AI and machine learning with NTA not only improves its adaptability but also strengthens its accuracy. AI algorithms become proficient at identifying novel attack vectors and complex evasion strategies that traditional security systems could miss as they continuously learn and adapt to changing network behaviours. In the continuously changing arena of cyber threats, where attackers are continually coming up with new ways to exploit vulnerabilities, this proactive strategy is especially important.

Beyond threat detection, AI, machine learning, and NTA work in harmony. It includes predictive analytics, which uses past data to foresee prospective security breaches or performance problems and then takes preventative measures. Additionally, AI-driven NTA systems help to improve network architecture and resource allocation by spotting patterns and trends, which enhances user experiences and optimises network performance.

However, incorporating AI and machine learning into NTA also poses difficulties. The quality of training data has a significant impact on how accurate AI models perform, and attackers may try to manipulate these models by introducing harmful data or using deceptive methods. Additionally, privacy issues must be addressed because intensive data monitoring may infringe on people's right to privacy. The need to strike a balance between user privacy and good network security is constant.

Machine Learning in Network Traffic Analysis

Network traffic analysis has made great progress recently thanks to the fusion of cutting-edge developments in artificial intelligence (AI), machine learning (ML), and network security. The monitoring and analysis of data packets as they move through computer networks in search of dangers, patterns, and anomalies constitutes network traffic analysis. Machine learning has completely changed this field because of its capacity to process and learn from enormous amounts of data.

A holistic approach to network traffic analysis is provided by AI and ML algorithms. The detection of online threats and intrusions is a prominent application. Because cyberattacks are constantly developing, conventional rule-based systems frequently find it difficult to stay up. On the other hand, ML systems can be trained to spot intricate attack patterns and abnormalities that might otherwise go undetected. In order to create models that can predict and stop possible security breaches, they analyse previous data, improving the overall network security posture.

Additionally, through anomaly detection, AI-driven network traffic analysis enables the discovery of fresh, undiscovered threats. ML models can detect deviations from the baseline of typical network behaviour that might point to a security breach or other questionable activity by creating a baseline of typical network behaviour. This preventative strategy aids in prompt response to new threats and lessens the effect of cyber catastrophes.

Additionally, real-time monitoring capabilities are improved with the addition of AI and ML to network security. Security teams can quickly discover and neutralise potential attacks because to the real-time processing and analysis of massive volumes of network data made possible by these technologies. This is especially important in the fast-paced digital environment of today, where immediate threat identification and action are critical.

It's important to recognise the difficulties that this integration presents, though. Large amounts of training data are necessary for ML models, and keeping datasets current is crucial to ensuring their accuracy. Additionally, adversarial attacks targeted at deceiving ML models raise serious issues for network security. Attackers may use flaws in ML algorithms to modify network traffic in an effort to avoid detection.

Case Study: Detecting DDoS Attacks

The detection of Distributed Denial of Service (DDoS) assaults has become a crucial topic of focus in the world of cutting-edge developments in AI, machine learning, and network security. Service interruptions, downtime, and significant financial losses can result from DDoS assaults, which are planned by malevolent actors to overwhelm a target system with a massive flow of traffic. The intricacy and size of these threats frequently make it difficult for traditional security measures to keep up, necessitating a more intelligent and dynamic approach.

This is where artificial intelligence and machine learning have revolutionised the detection of DDoS attacks. Researchers and security specialists are now able to create models that can quickly analyse huge amounts of network data in real time by utilising the power of cutting-edge algorithms and deep learning techniques. Even in the face of attack techniques that are continually developing, these models are able to distinguish between legitimate user traffic and malicious requests.

Traditional rule-based systems may fail to detect zero-day attacks due to the limitations of machine learning algorithms' capacity to learn from past data and adapt to new attack patterns. These algorithms have the ability to independently detect anomalies in network traffic, such as unexpected spikes or odd patterns, and initiate prompt actions to lessen the effects of the assault. Additionally, AI-driven systems can provide predictive capabilities, anticipating potential weaknesses and proactively boosting defences.

These developments have also led to the emergence of cooperative defence mechanisms. Platforms powered by AI can connect with one another, exchanging real-time threat information and collaborating to strengthen their defences. This degree of cooperation improves networks' overall resistance to DDoS attacks by building a strong ecosystem that enables speedy detection, isolation, and neutralisation of attacks.

Although these cutting-edge technologies show great potential, there are still problems. To keep up with new attack tactics, the models must be continuously updated and trained. Furthermore, it is crucial to ensure the ethical usage of AI and protect against false positives in order to avoid legitimate user traffic being mistakenly labelled as malicious.

Finally, the integration of AI, machine learning, and network security is revolutionising DDoS assault detection. Organisations may improve their capacity to fend off attacks, reduce downtime, and protect the integrity of their digital infrastructure by utilising these ground-breaking developments. This multifaceted strategy serves as a beacon of resilience in an increasingly linked and precarious digital world as dangers continue to evolve.

Visualizing Results

The landscape of technology and information protection has undergone a considerable transformation in recent years as a result of inventive developments in AI, machine learning, and network security. The capacity to visualise outcomes effectively is one of the crucial factors influencing these shifts. The ability to communicate nuanced patterns, trends, and insights produced from sizable datasets and complex algorithms has been greatly improved by the use of visualisation tools.

The visualisation of findings is vital for model interpretation, validation, and improvement in the field of AI and machine learning. Understanding the reasoning behind these models' judgements has grown more difficult with the emergence of deep learning architectures and complex neural networks. Researchers and practitioners can explore model behaviour using visualisation tools to spot key characteristics and areas of influence. This helps identify biases and improves model transparency, assuring ethical AI deployment. Additionally, visualisations aid in communicating AI-generated results to stakeholders who are not technically savvy, bridging the knowledge gap between specialists and decision-makers.

The visualisation of results has also considerably improved network security. Security experts use AI-driven algorithms to find anomalies and potential breaches as cyber-attacks become more advanced. Visualisations help in illustrating the patterns of network traffic and spotting odd spikes or activity that can point to an ongoing attack. Security teams can respond quickly and put preventative measures in place to fend off any threats by recognising these trends. Furthermore, organisations can more effectively allocate resources by prioritising areas that need urgent attention with the aid of visual representations of security postures and vulnerabilities.

Interactive and dynamic visualisation tools have been developed as a result of innovations in this area of AI, machine learning, and network security. Real-time monitoring and analysis made possible by these instruments enables quicker decision-making and adaptable responses to new threats. Additionally, visualisation has enabled the gamification of security training, which has improved cybersecurity workers' skill sets and better prepared them for the always changing threat scenario.

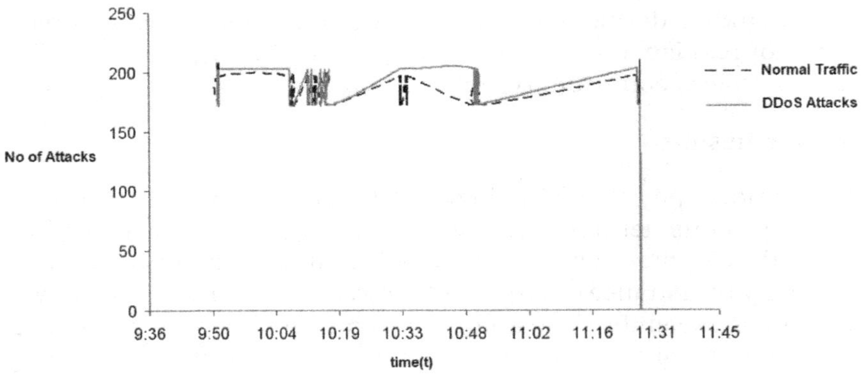

Graph: Normal Traffic and DDoS Attack Traffic

Code Example: Implementing Network Traffic Analysis

```
from sklearn.ensemble import RandomForestClassifier
from sklearn.model_selection import train_test_split
from sklearn.metrics import accuracy_score

# Load and preprocess dataset
# ...

# Split dataset
X_train, X_test, y_train, y_test = train_test_split(features, labels,
test_size=0.2, random_state=42)

# Initialize Random Forest classifier
model = RandomForestClassifier()

# Train the model
model.fit(X_train, y_train)

# Predict on test data
predictions = model.predict(X_test)
```

```
# Evaluate accuracy
accuracy = accuracy_score(y_test, predictions)
print("Model Accuracy:", accuracy)
```

Conclusion

AI and machine learning-powered network traffic analysis is a crucial tool for spotting suspicious patterns and boosting network security. Real-time anomaly detection enables a proactive approach to cybersecurity that protects digital assets and guarantees the unhindered flow of information.

5.5 PREDICTIVE ANALYSIS OF CYBERATTACKS AND VULNERABILITY MANAGEMENT

Traditional reactive strategies are no longer adequate in the constantly changing field of cybersecurity to safeguard sensitive digital assets. Artificial intelligence (AI) and machine learning (ML)-powered predictive analysis has emerged as a paradigm shift in cyber defence. This chapter examines the subtleties of predictive analysis in cyberattacks and vulnerability management, illuminating how these ground-breaking methods can proactively counter threats and improve network security.

Understanding Predictive Analysis in Cybersecurity

A new use of cutting-edge developments in AI, machine learning, and network security is predictive analysis in cybersecurity. It entails using these technologies to their full potential to foresee potential cyber threats and thwart them before they become actual attacks. AI and machine learning algorithms can find patterns, anomalies, and trends by examining enormous amounts of historical data that would otherwise be invisible to human analysts. Organisations may keep ahead of new threats by proactively detecting vulnerabilities and potential attack vectors thanks to this predictive capacity. Continuous model adaptation and improvement enabled by machine learning algorithms ensures a flexible and current defence plan.

By learning from previously observed behaviours, cutting-edge AI-driven systems can anticipate new, previously undiscovered dangers in addition to well-known attack routes. To produce thorough risk evaluations, these systems may analyse data from a variety of sources, including network traffic, user behaviour, system logs, and even external threat intelligence feeds. In order to efficiently prioritise and deploy resources and handle the most urgent risks, organisations can benefit from this. This preventative strategy shortens response times and lessens the potential harm that hackers may do.

Predictive analysis has significant advantages for network security as well. AI-powered intrusion detection systems can quickly identify possible breaches by spotting suspicious activity in real time. These systems can offer a more accurate risk assessment and aid in creating stronger defence plans by continuously learning from changing attack methodologies. Predictive analysis can also help automate procedures for incident response, ensuring that the right steps are taken right away in the event of an attack.

Machine Learning Algorithms for Predictive Analysis

In the fields of cutting-edge developments in artificial intelligence, machine learning, and network security, predictive analysis utilising machine learning algorithms has emerged as a transformational force. These algorithms have completely changed how businesses and scholars approach difficult problems. Predictive analysis uses techniques like deep learning neural networks, recurrent neural networks, and transformers in the field of AI and machine learning to forecast future trends, events, and behaviours based on historical data. Applications made possible by this include tailored recommendation systems, medical diagnosis, and financial market forecasts.

Additionally, the combination of network security and machine intelligence has significantly improved the protection of digital ecosystems. Support vector machines, random forests, and convolutional neural networks are just a few of the algorithms used by intrusion detection systems today to spot suspicious activity in networks and stop cyberattacks before they can do any damage. These algorithms can adapt to changing threats and analyse trends in real-time network traffic data to provide a proactive defence against complex attacks.

Cutting-edge breakthroughs like autonomous threat hunting, where AI algorithms autonomously search networks to find concealed weaknesses and prospective breaches, are the result of the synergy of predictive analysis, AI, machine learning, and network security. Additionally, the 'black-box' problem has been solved by the creation of explainable AI algorithms, improving transparency and accountability in AI-driven decision-making processes.

Predictive Analysis Workflow

In the field of cutting-edge developments in AI, machine learning, and network security, predictive analysis has become a crucial element. In this multidimensional approach, previous data and patterns are meticulously analysed in order to predict future trends, behaviours, and potential security concerns. Organisations may gain useful insights from massive datasets by utilising the power of AI and machine learning algorithms, empowering them to make educated decisions and develop proactive strategies.

The data collection and preprocessing phase of the workflow is where a variety of data streams are often obtained from different sources, such as network logs, user actions, and system behaviours. To assure the quality and usefulness of the raw data for analysis, it is then cleaned, normalised, and transformed. Then, to find underlying patterns and connections in the data, machine learning methods are used, including regression, time-series analysis, and classification models.

Deep learning methods like neural networks are being used to handle more complicated and unstructured data as AI development moves forward, improving prediction accuracy. Predictive analysis can help in the early discovery of abnormalities or potential cyber threats in network security, for example, by identifying departures from established patterns.

Additionally, the combination of AI-driven technologies like natural language processing and predictive analytics makes it easier to extract insights from textual data, which leads to a more thorough understanding of changing trends. This is especially important when using sentiment analysis to gauge public opinion because it can affect how decisions are made across a variety of fields.

This workflow's model training and validation phase is crucial. By separating historical data into training and testing sets, models are able to learn from the past and evaluate their predictive power against yet-unknown data. Models are refined iteratively to increase their effectiveness and generalizability.

Predictive analysis is essential for identifying prospective weaknesses in network security and creating preventative actions. Organisations can predict potential security gaps and take proactive measures to protect their networks by analysing previous breach data and attack routes. Additionally, the incorporation of real-time data streams makes it possible to spot emerging risks and take prompt action, strengthening overall cybersecurity tactics.

Visualization and Interpretability

Innovative developments in network security, machine learning, and artificial intelligence are driven in large part by interpretability and visualisation. Complex models, such as deep neural networks, have demonstrated extraordinary ability in the field of AI and machine learning, yet they frequently lack transparency. Through the use of visualisation tools, academics and practitioners can learn more about these models' inner workings and how decisions are made. Building trust, identifying faults, and improving model performance all depend on this.

On the other hand, interpretability concentrates on making model outputs comprehensible to human users. Understanding the logic behind decisions becomes crucial as AI systems are increasingly incorporated into crucial applications like healthcare diagnosis or autonomous vehicles. By enabling users to understand and trust AI judgements through interpretability techniques like feature importance visualisation or producing human-readable explanations for model predictions, these technologies become more morally acceptable and more frequently used.

Visualisation and interpretability are advantageous for network security, another area where AI has a huge impact. Massive volumes of data are processed by AI-driven security systems in order to identify and address risks. Security analysts can grasp the changing threat landscape, comprehend attack patterns, and monitor potential vulnerabilities in real-time thanks to transparent visualisation tools. Security specialists can accurately assess the veracity of alarms by understanding the outputs of AI models and swiftly take the necessary action to stop suspected breaches or assaults.

New visualisation methods and interpretability frameworks are directly related to the development of novel developments in these disciplines. Researchers are constantly developing techniques that can offer clear, practical insights into the intricate inner workings of AI models. These developments make sure that AI and machine learning systems are more approachable, accountable, and in line with human values by striking a balance between predictive capability and interpretability. This in turn promotes responsible adoption and supports continuous advancements in network security, AI, and machine learning.

Case Study: Predicting DDoS Attacks

In recent years, significant developments in AI, machine learning, and network security have been integrated to strengthen digital infrastructures in response to the increasing frequency and sophistication of Distributed Denial of Service (DDoS) assaults. These assaults, which aim to overwhelm a target system or network with an excessive amount of data, can cause significant downtime and cost organisations money. Researchers and cybersecurity specialists have used cutting-edge technologies to forecast and mitigate DDoS attacks in real-time in order to combat this danger.

Artificial intelligence (AI) and machine learning algorithms have demonstrated their value in spotting patterns and abnormalities that human monitoring may miss. These technologies are able to identify minute differences from expected behaviour, which may be signs of an oncoming DDoS attack, by analysing enormous amounts of network traffic data. These algorithms improve their accuracy over time by learning to distinguish between legal traffic and fraudulent requests using past data. Additionally, AI-driven systems provide a more proactive defence mechanism by adapting to changing assault techniques.

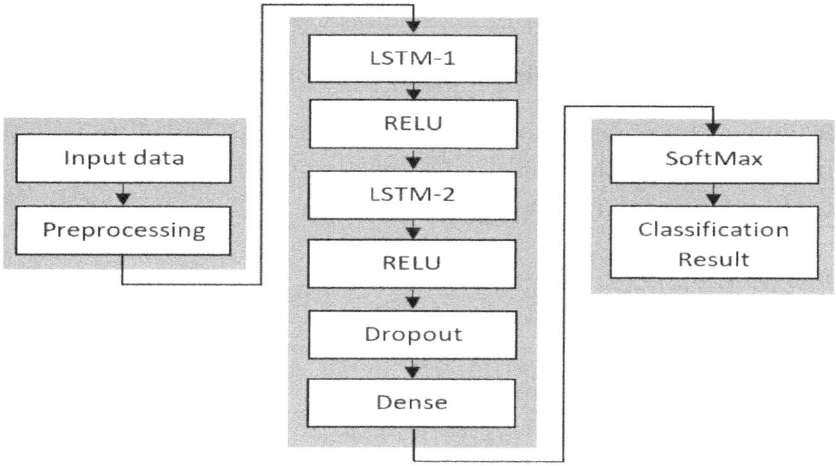

Figure 3: LSTM Predictions for DDoS Attacks

The implementation of intelligent intrusion detection and prevention systems is required for the integration of network security with AI and machine learning. These programmes continuously scan network activity to spot odd traffic patterns. They are capable of identifying zero-day attacks, which are exploits aimed at flaws the system's developers are unaware of. These solutions provide a quicker response, reducing the impact of DDoS attacks, by being able to spot even tiny variations from normal network behaviour.

Real-time adaptive mitigation strategies are also improved in this area. These methods use AI algorithms to dynamically reroute traffic, separate genuine from fraudulent requests, and optimally deploy resources to maintain service. This adaptability is essential for managing abrupt, enormous traffic spikes during DDoS attacks.

Despite the advancements, problems still exist. AI is also being used by adversaries to create increasingly complex attacks that may be able to get past conventional defences. In this game of cat and mouse, defence tactics must constantly change. The ethical application of AI in cybersecurity also prompts worries about potential false positives and the privacy implications.

Conclusion

In terms of cyber defence, predictive analysis represents a considerable advancement. Organisations can foresee cyber risks and take preventative action to protect their digital assets by utilising the potential of AI and ML. Predictive analysis will surely be crucial in creating robust cybersecurity tactics as threats continue to evolve.

Code Example: Implementing Random Forest for Predictive Analysis

```
from sklearn.ensemble import RandomForestClassifier
from sklearn.model_selection import train_test_split
from sklearn.metrics import accuracy_score

# Load preprocessed dataset
X, y = load_preprocessed_data()

# Split dataset into training and testing sets
X_train, X_test, y_train, y_test = train_test_split(X, y, test_size=0.2,
random_state=42)

# Initialize Random Forest classifier
rf_classifier = RandomForestClassifier(n_estimators=100, random_
state=42)

# Train the classifier
rf_classifier.fit(X_train, y_train)
```

```
# Make predictions
predictions = rf_classifier.predict(X_test)

# Calculate accuracy
accuracy = accuracy_score(y_test, predictions)
print(f"Accuracy: {accuracy:.2f}")
```

5.6 AI-ENHANCED INCIDENT RESPONSE AND FORENSICS

With the incorporation of artificial intelligence (AI) and machine learning (ML) tools, the subject of cybersecurity has recently undergone a profound transformation. Incident response and digital forensics have been significantly impacted by this trend, allowing organisations to effectively combat and manage the increasingly complex nature of cyber threats. In this chapter, we explore the approaches, advantages, difficulties, and prospects of AI-enhanced incident response and forensics.

The Intersection of AI, Machine Learning, and Cybersecurity

The sciences of artificial intelligence, machine learning, and cybersecurity have improved tremendously as a result of the convergence of these three fields. The protection of digital assets and the fight against cyber threats are being revolutionised by AI-powered solutions as a result of this confluence.

AI and machine learning are being used to improve threat identification and response in the field of cybersecurity. Traditional rule-based strategies are constrained by their incapacity to change to new assault methods. AI-driven models, on the other hand, are able to analyse enormous amounts of data in real-time, spotting patterns and anomalies that could indicate future breaches or assaults. These technologies can quickly identify hazards that were previously undetected, speeding up response times and enabling preventative steps.

Additionally, machine learning algorithms are essential for creating predictive analytics, which enables businesses to anticipate possible weaknesses based on historical data. This helps with risk evaluation and resource allocation, sharpening and streamlining network security tactics.

AI is also being used to create increasingly sophisticated strikes on the offensive side. This necessitates a defensive reaction that uses the same technology for defence. The cybersecurity industry is investing in ethical hacking and penetration testing powered by AI to find vulnerabilities before criminal actors can take advantage of them. A dynamic and changing environment is being created by the hostile usage of AI that is forcing defenders to constantly improve their security protocols.

However, there are obstacles to overcome in order to fully integrate AI and machine learning into cybersecurity. The privacy of sensitive data used to train AI models must be protected, and algorithmic bias must be avoided. Additionally, security professionals must always refresh their skills and equipment due to the quick evolution of AI-powered threats.

AI-enhanced Incident Response

One of the most revolutionary applications of cutting-edge developments in AI, machine learning, and network security is the incorporation of AI-enhanced incident response. since of the constantly changing nature of cyber threats, traditional incident response techniques frequently found it difficult to keep up since the sheer volume and complexity of attacks might be overwhelming for human responders. However, a paradigm shift in how organisations identify, assess, and respond to security issues has happened as a result of the integration of AI and machine learning technology.

Artificial intelligence (AI)-enhanced incident response makes use of the capabilities of machine learning algorithms to quickly analyse massive amounts of data produced across networked systems. This involves the continuous observation of system operations, log files, user behaviour, and network traffic. Through ongoing analysis, AI models can quickly spot anomalies that could be signs of possible security breaches or unauthorised activity while also learning the baseline patterns of typical network activity inside an organisation.

Additionally, incident response technologies powered by AI are able to contextualise and prioritise security issues according to their seriousness and potential impact. These systems can assist human responders in making better decisions by helping them comprehend the context. This helps them allocate resources more effectively and address the most urgent threats first. A more flexible and responsive security posture is the outcome of this combination of human expertise and AI-driven insights.

The potential of AI-enhanced incident response to adapt and learn from new data is particularly novel. AI models may be updated to recognise new attack pathways and strategies as cyberthreats change. Organisations are better able to keep ahead of hackers and successfully address never-before-seen risks thanks to this dynamic learning process.

While AI-driven incident response has many advantages, there are still difficulties. As adversaries can try to modify these models to avoid detection, protecting the integrity and security of the AI models themselves is essential. Since AI systems' automated decision-making processes must adhere to legal and regulatory frameworks, ethical considerations are also relevant.

AI-enhanced Digital Forensics

The fields of artificial intelligence, machine learning, and network security come together in a revolutionary way in AI-enhanced digital forensics to completely change the way cyber investigations and threat reduction are conducted. This paradigm change makes it possible for digital forensic professionals to quickly analyse and comprehend complex patterns inside enormous datasets that were previously insurmountable by utilising the huge processing capacity of AI. These systems are equipped with machine learning algorithms, which have been refined through intensive training on historical cyber occurrences. These algorithms enable them to detect anomalies, spot possible dangers, and even forecast future intrusions with a high degree of accuracy.

This innovation's capacity to manage the explosive expansion of digital evidence in the linked world of today is one of its most enticing features. The sheer volume and complexity of data collected across many platforms made it difficult for traditional methods of digital forensics to keep up. AI serves as a force multiplier in this situation, quickly sifting through masses of data to find hidden signs of hostile activity, unauthorised access, or data breaches. Investigators can focus their skills on more strategic and complex areas of cybercrime investigation by automating typical operations like evidence gathering, data analysis, and correlation.

Furthermore, AI holds the possibility of proactive defence, going beyond retrospective analysis in the context of digital forensics. Machine learning models that have been trained on past attack patterns can forecast network vulnerabilities and suggest preventative ways to strengthen the security posture of the system. The incidence and effects of cyber disasters could be considerably reduced by this switch from reactive to proactive methods.

However, AI-enhanced digital forensics has its own set of problems, just like any other transformational technology. Critical issues that necessitate careful consideration include the dependability of AI-driven choices, the transparency of algorithmic procedures, and the possibility of adversarial attacks on AI systems. Additionally, to ensure that AI models are successful against new attack vectors, ongoing upgrades and enhancements are required due to the always changing nature of cyber threats.

Challenges and Future Directions

The fields of artificial intelligence, machine learning, and network security have made incredible strides in recent years that have changed both companies and civilizations. But these successes also bring a number of difficulties and a variety of future prospects, which call for careful thought and creative answers.

The problem of bias and fairness is one of the biggest problems in the field of AI and machine learning. The risk of maintaining societal biases grows as AI systems increasingly have a say in important decisions like hiring, lending, and law enforcement. Future efforts in this regard include cultivating inclusive and varied training datasets, adopting rigorous bias detection and mitigation techniques, and creating more reliable and interpretable AI models.

The issue of data privacy and security has become more pressing as a result of the exponential growth in AI and machine learning applications. Given how strongly these systems rely on data, finding a balance between protecting private data and maintaining effective learning opportunities is still a challenge. The field's future depends on developing machine learning algorithms that respect user privacy, utilising methods like federated learning, and abiding by changing data protection laws.

In the age of linked gadgets and the Internet of Things (IoT), network security faces growing dangers. Networks are more vulnerable to cyberattacks as a result of weaknesses being amplified by network complexity. The development of adaptive and self-learning security mechanisms that can foresee and mitigate new threats in real-time, as well as the incorporation of AI-driven anomaly detection systems to spot unusual patterns suggestive of prospective assaults, will be priorities for future work.

Additionally, the development of AI has helped to raise the level of sophistication in cyberattacks. An important issue is adversarial attacks, in which malevolent actors meticulously create inputs to manipulate AI systems. Future directions involve building strong AI models that are resistant to such assaults, necessitating a greater comprehension of adversary weaknesses and the creation of efficient defences.

It is essential to work together and conduct multidisciplinary study to address these issues and determine future course. The formation of standards for responsible AI deployment, transparency in algorithmic decision-making, and ethical issues related to the use of AI are other crucial issues that must be thoroughly addressed.

Conclusion

With previously unheard-of speed, precision, and scale, AI and ML have completely changed the incident response and forensics scene. These technologies do not, however, come without difficulties. Maximising the advantages of AI in the field of cybersecurity will require striking a balance between automation and human skill.

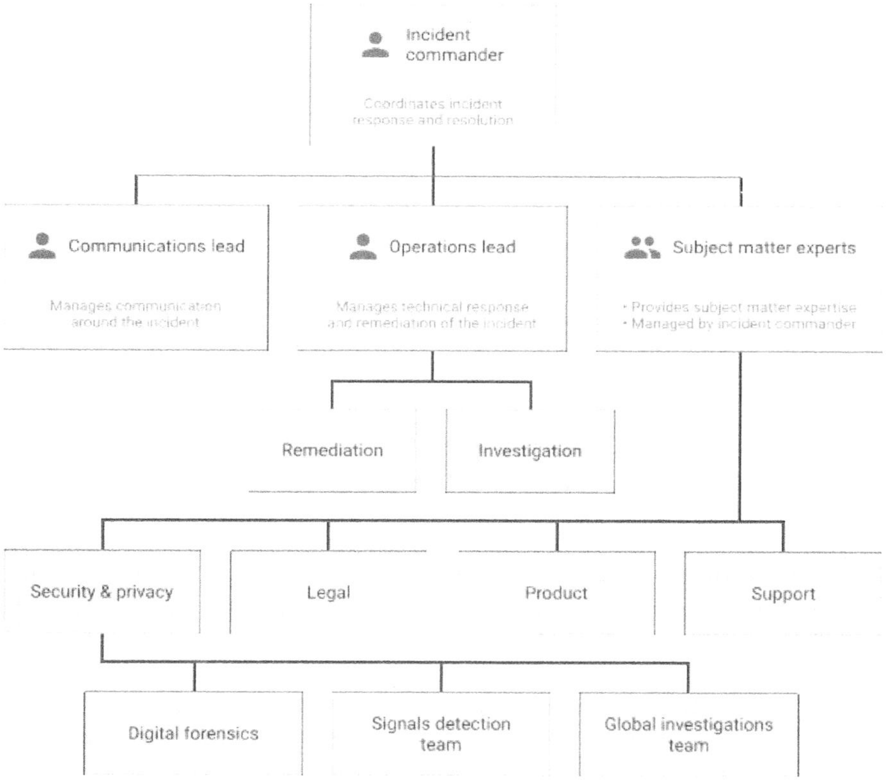

Figure 4: Incident Response Workflow

Table 3: Comparison of Traditional vs. AI-enhanced Incident Response

Aspect	Traditional Approach	AI-enhanced Approach
Speed of Analysis	Slower	Real-time
Human Intervention	High	Reduced
Scalability	Limited	High
Anomaly Detection	Rule-based	Data-driven

5.7 THREAT INTELLIGENCE SHARING AND COLLABORATIVE DEFENSE

Organisations face an ever-increasing volume and sophistication of cyber threats in the quickly changing world of cybersecurity. Threat actors are always coming up with new ways to hack systems, steal data, and interfere with operations. In response, the cybersecurity community has realised how crucial it is to work together and share knowledge in order to effectively combat these threats. In-depth discussion of the idea of threat intelligence sharing and collaborative defence is provided in this chapter, along with an examination of its importance, difficulties, and how AI and machine learning might improve these practises.

Understanding Threat Intelligence Sharing

Threat Intelligence Sharing represents a critical paradigm shift in how organisations approach the always changing spectrum of cybersecurity threats. It is at the forefront of revolutionary breakthroughs in AI, machine learning, and network security. Threat intelligence in this sense refers to the collected, organised, and analysed data about possible and actual cyberthreats, including their methods, telltale signs, causes, and targets. The way threat intelligence is gathered, processed, and used has been revolutionised by the incorporation of AI and machine learning technology. These cutting-edge methods allow for the automatic analysis of enormous volumes of data, spotting patterns and abnormalities that could elude human observation and allowing for a more timely and precise reaction to potential threats.

A thorough awareness of the threat landscape is also possible thanks to the quick correlation of various types of threat intelligence data by AI and machine learning algorithms. This comprehensive understanding improves the accuracy of predictive modelling, allowing businesses to foresee future attack pathways and weaknesses. A more adaptable and responsive security posture is ensured by AI-driven systems, which can learn from previous data to adapt their models to new threat kinds and developing strategies.

However, the collaborative aspect of threat intelligence sharing is what will really transform the game. The hitherto segregated approach to cybersecurity is insufficient given the growth of linked systems. Organisations today understand the importance of working together to keep one step ahead of cyber threats. In terms of network security, this is where AI and machine learning excel. These solutions can combine and anonymize threat data from several sources, allowing for information sharing without jeopardising sensitive data. Organisations may strengthen their defences jointly by establishing a community-driven approach to threat intelligence, utilising shared insights to identify emerging threats and develop efficient remedies.

As a result, organisations are now better equipped to preventatively protect their digital assets because to the groundbreaking synergy created by the combination of threat intelligence sharing, AI, machine learning, and network security. This combination not only strengthens individual security postures but also improves the global cybersecurity ecosystem, fostering a cooperative setting that jointly counters cyber threats. This integration will probably continue to be a pillar in the ongoing conflict with increasingly capable cyber enemies as technology develops.

Collaborative Defense and its Mechanisms

As AI, machine learning, and network security continue to progress, collaborative defence has become a crucial tactic. Traditional security measures frequently fall short in effectively thwarting sophisticated cyber assaults in a digital environment that is becoming more interconnected. This problem is addressed by collaborative defence, which promotes cooperation among a variety of parties, including businesses, cybersecurity professionals, AI developers, and law enforcement agencies. This strategy is predicated on the idea that pooling threat intelligence, examining attack trends, and jointly creating AI-driven remedies will improve the state of overall security.

At its foundation, collaborative defence makes use of artificial intelligence (AI) and machine learning to proactively identify, assess, and react to threats. These tools can comb through enormous amounts of data, picking out anomalies and patterns that could otherwise go undiscovered. Participating entities can contribute insights from their various points of view collectively through shared threat intelligence platforms, enhancing the collective understanding of new threats and attack vectors. The creation of more reliable and flexible defence measures is made possible by this cooperative ecosystem.

Additionally, collective defence encourages the development of AI-driven solutions that improve threat detection while automating response processes. Machine learning algorithms can use historical attack data to identify potential risks in the future, allowing for more rapid and precise decision-making. To reduce the potential impact of cyberattacks, real-time information exchange and coordinated incident response enable a more flexible defence posture.

However, there are difficulties in putting collaborative defence into practise. Three crucial difficulties that must be addressed are participant trust, data privacy issues, and the requirement for standardised information exchange procedures. Additionally, to keep up with new threats, defensive measures must be constantly updated due to the quick development of AI and machine learning approaches.

AI and Machine Learning in Threat Intelligence

Recent developments in network security and the general cybersecurity landscape have resulted from the application of AI and machine learning (ML) techniques to the field of threat intelligence. The detection, analysis, and response of organisations to emerging cyber threats have been profoundly altered by this convergence.

The sheer volume, velocity, and complexity of contemporary cyber threats have shown to be particularly well-suited for AI and ML technologies to handle. These tools can find patterns, anomalies, and connections through the examination of enormous datasets that could go undetected by humans. The time it takes to identify and address potential security breaches is decreased because to this technology, which enables more precise and proactive threat identification.

Predictive analytics is a significant area where AI and ML are being used in threat intelligence. These technologies can foresee potential future attacks by examining historical data and spotting trends, assisting organisations in formulating effective defence strategies. Aside from automating the process of gathering, curating, and contextualising threat data from diverse sources, AI-driven threat intelligence solutions may also give security professionals thorough insights and liberate them from time-consuming manual duties.

The advancements in AI and ML have benefitted network security particularly. These innovations enable intrusion detection systems to develop greater adaptability and self-learning capabilities. They assist separate real threats from false positives by being able to discriminate between legitimate network activity and malicious activity. AI-driven threat hunting can also spot cutting-edge attack methods that get past conventional signature-based defences.

However, there are difficulties associated with this integration. The success of the technology is greatly influenced by the calibre and volume of the training data, and adversaries are quick to change their strategies to avoid being detected by AI-based defences. Furthermore, there are still major questions about the interpretability and openness of AI-generated insights, particularly in high-stakes situations when it is important to understand the decision-making process.

Case Study: AI-Enhanced Threat Intelligence Platform

The case study "AI-Enhanced Threat Intelligence Platform in Innovative Advancements in AI, Machine Learning, and Network Security" explores the transformative nexus of network security, artificial intelligence (AI), and machine learning (ML) as they relate to threat intelligence. Traditional security measures frequently fall short in today's fast changing digital environment, where cyber-attacks are more sophisticated and prevalent than ever. This case study investigates how utilising AI and ML technologies has produced a state-of-the-art Threat Intelligence Platform (TIP) that enables organisations to proactively discover, assess, and mitigate possible security threats.

This platform makes use of AI to automate threat detection and analysis procedures, cutting down on the time needed for human intervention and reaction. The TIP can learn and adapt to new attack vectors and techniques thanks to machine learning algorithms that have been trained on enormous datasets of historical threat information. This improves the TIP's predictive capabilities. The discovery of subtle patterns and anomalies that might elude conventional security systems is also aided by adaptive learning, offering a thorough defence mechanism.

Additionally, the use of AI-driven NLP makes it easier to extract useful insights in real-time from sources of unstructured data, such as security blogs, forums, and social media. This improves the platform's ability to provide actionable intelligence about new threats and weaknesses. The TIP's capacity to contextualise and correlate threat data from diverse sources improves its accuracy in assessing the seriousness and veracity of prospective hazards.

The case study highlights the platform's continual improvement cycle as one of its notable benefits. The algorithms in the TIP improve as fresh data and experiences are processed, improving threat detection and reducing false positives. This self-learning system is evidence of the continual progress in AI and ML that makes it possible to develop flexible and adaptable security solutions.

The case study emphasises how the convergence of AI, ML, and network security has produced an AI-Enhanced Threat Intelligence Platform in its conclusion. By offering proactive, intelligent, and context-aware threat detection and analysis, this platform shows how cutting-edge technologies have the ability to completely transform the cybersecurity industry. This AI-powered technology offers a strong line of defence against evolving cyber threats, assisting organisations in staying one step ahead of their attackers in an increasingly complicated digital environment.

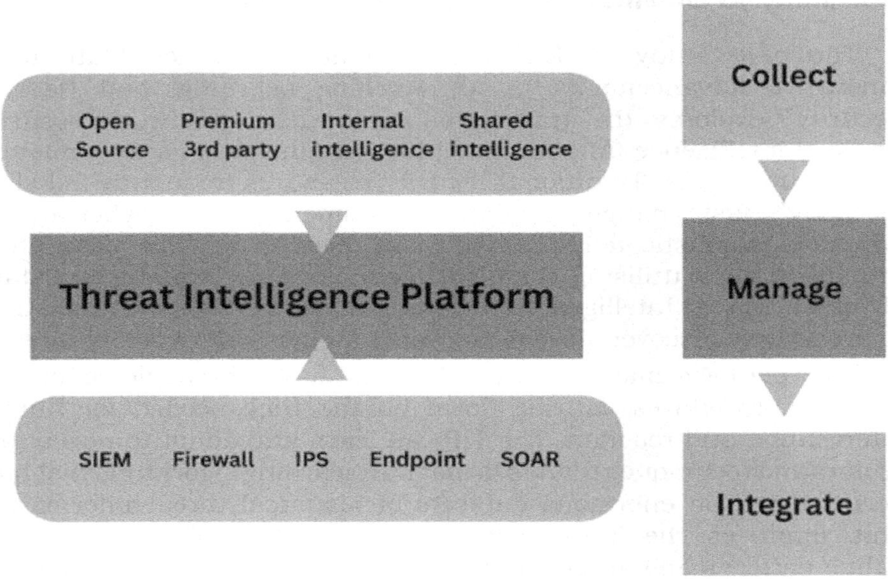

Figure 5: Threat Intelligence Platform Architecture

Conclusion

In today's cybersecurity environment, cooperative defence and the sharing of threat intelligence are essential tactics. The tools to process and analyse the massive amounts of threat data are provided by AI and machine learning technologies, allowing organisations to collaborate to defend against cyber threats. The cybersecurity community can create a more robust and integrated defence ecosystem by adopting these techniques and tools.

5.8 MACHINE LEARNING IN EMAIL SECURITY AND PHISHING DETECTION

Email communication has become a vital component of our personal and professional life in a world that is becoming more and more digital. However, there are risks associated with this convenience, particularly when it comes to phishing assaults. Phishing attacks include fraudsters sending phoney emails to victims in an effort to trick them into disclosing personal data like passwords or credit card numbers. In the field of email security, machine learning (ML) has become a potent tool for phishing attack detection and mitigation. The use of machine learning algorithms for email security and phishing detection is examined in this chapter.

Understanding Phishing Attacks

The article "Phishing Attacks in Innovative Advancements in AI, Machine Learning, and Network Security" discusses the changing cyber threat landscape and the accompanying defensive strategies that make use of cutting-edge technologies. AI and machine learning are always improving, and so are the methods used by bad actors. Through the use of these cutting-edge technology, phishing attacks, a well-known and widespread type of cybercrime, have undergone a change.

In order to create more convincing phishing messages and improve the targeting of potential victims, AI and machine learning techniques are being used. Due to these developments, hackers are now able to analyse massive quantities of data to produce personalised, contextually appropriate phishing emails that are more likely to trick their intended targets. Additionally, automation backed by AI enables attackers to extend their operations effectively, casting a larger net for potential victims.

The same technologies that give attackers more power, meanwhile, also present viable remedies. Utilising pattern recognition and anomaly detection, AI and machine learning can be used for proactive threat detection, identifying suspicious behaviours suggestive of phishing efforts. These technologies are being included into network security protocols to quickly identify and respond to new threats, closing the window of vulnerability.

Cybercriminals and cybersecurity experts are always developing more advanced methods as a result of the ongoing arms competition. A dynamic cycle of attack and defence is being played out as AI and machine learning become more integrated into both sides of this battle. The development of phishing assaults in this setting emphasises how crucial it is for network security to constantly adapt and innovate. In the end, how to strike a balance between securing digital ecosystems and the persistence of cyber threats will depend on how human expertise works with AI and machine learning skills.

Machine Learning in Phishing Detection

In order to strengthen defences, innovative developments in artificial intelligence (AI), machine learning (ML), and network security have been explored in recent years due to the growing threat of cyberattacks, notably phishing. Phishing, a deceptive tactic used by malevolent actors to fool people into disclosing sensitive information or committing destructive acts, has advanced, calling for the creation of more effective countermeasures. In order to develop more proactive and efficient systems for detecting and mitigating phishing attacks, network security protocols have been combined with AI and ML techniques in response to this problem.

Machine learning has become a key component in the detection of phishing due to its ability to process massive volumes of data and identify trends. ML algorithms can learn to recognise common traits and small variances suggestive of fraudulent activities by analysing historical phishing attack data. In order to keep up with fraudsters, these algorithms can then be trained to recognise new and emerging phishing techniques. By analysing the content of phishing emails and comparing it to established patterns of legitimate correspondence, techniques like natural language processing (NLP) are used to help the system flag questionable messages.

Additionally, the incorporation of AI strengthens these initiatives by enabling systems to make quick judgements based on shifting threat scenarios. To improve detection accuracy and lower false positives, AI-driven models can use contextual data such as user behaviour patterns and network anomalies. AI also makes it possible for automatic reactions and mitigation techniques, which successfully eliminate potential dangers before they may do harm.

Innovations in this area go beyond simple detection to include preventative interventions. By examining past data and finding new attack vectors, predictive analytics, a subset of AI and ML, may forecast possible phishing trends and weaknesses. Organisations are able to strengthen their defences proactively thanks to this foresight, keeping them one step ahead of attackers.

Case Study: PhishNet

Attacks including phishing have grown to be one of the most damaging and prevalent online hazards, affecting both people and businesses all over the world. The creation of cutting-edge solutions that integrate AI, machine learning, and network security has become crucial in response to this growing threat. The "PhishNet" case study serves as a shining illustration of how the fusion of these technologies might completely alter the cybersecurity landscape.

PhishNet, a state-of-the-art system that showcases cutting-edge innovations, uses AI and machine learning to proactively detect and stop phishing assaults. Traditional techniques for detecting phishing attempts frequently use static rule-based systems that find it difficult to keep up with the continually changing techniques used by hackers. On the other hand, PhishNet uses dynamic algorithms that continuously learn from new information and adapt, improving its accuracy and effectiveness over time.

Deep learning techniques are at the heart of PhishNet's analysis of huge datasets that include email headers, content, sender behaviour, and network properties. Due to this, the system is able to recognise small trends and abnormalities that may point to phishing attempts, even when covered in elaborate veneers. PhishNet can detect newly unknown approaches in addition to well-known phishing indications thanks to the incorporation of neural networks, keeping it one step ahead of online attacks.

It is important to note that PhishNet operates inside a larger framework for network security rather than independently. Cross-referencing its findings with real-time threat information feeds enhances its assessments and gives prospective threats context. This cooperative strategy not only improves the speed of risk reduction but also the accuracy of danger identification.

Additionally, PhishNet helps to build a community-wide defence against phishing attempts. Its observations are shared, anonymised, and incorporated into the defence mechanisms of other interconnected systems as it discovers new patterns and strategies. This strategy not only improves cybersecurity generally but also makes sure that AI's learning curve is exponential, reflecting the quick development of cyberthreats.

The PhishNet case study highlights the disruptive potential of combining network security, AI, and machine learning in the field of cybersecurity. PhishNet demonstrates how technology can be used to proactively combat the changing landscape of phishing assaults by taking a dynamic and learning-oriented strategy. Innovations like PhishNet show a future where adaptability and collaboration are essential to protecting digital ecosystems as cyber threats continue to become more complex.

Conclusion

By enabling more sophisticated phishing detection capabilities, machine learning has revolutionised email security. ML-driven systems like PhishNet provide a proactive defence against phishing attempts as cyber threats become more complex, protecting people and organisations from the terrible effects of cybercrime.

Table 4: Comparison of ML Algorithms for Phishing Detection

Algorithm	Pros	Cons
Random Forests	Handles categorical data	Limited capability with image analysis
Neural Networks	Learns intricate patterns	Requires substantial computational resources
Support Vector Machines	Effective in high-dimensional spaces	Slower training time for large datasets

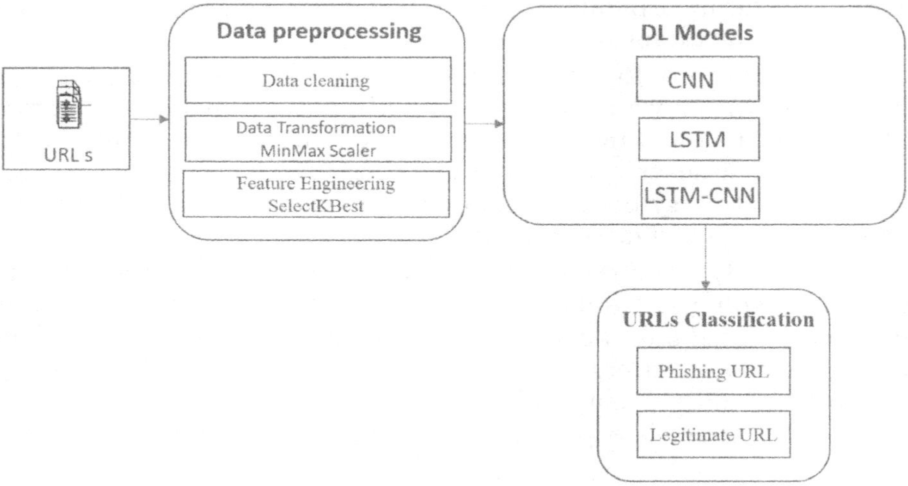

Figure 6: CNN Architecture in Phishing Detection

Graph: Phishing Sites Detected - 2022

Code Example:Text Feature Extraction using TF-IDF in Python

```
from sklearn.feature_extraction.text import TfidfVectorizer

# Sample email content
email_content = ["Greetings! Please update your password.", "URGENT: Your account has been compromised."]

# Create TF-IDF vectorizer
vectorizer = TfidfVectorizer()
tfidf_matrix = vectorizer.fit_transform(email_content)

# Extract feature names
feature_names = vectorizer.get_feature_names_out()

# Display TF-IDF features
print(feature_names)
```

5.9 AI-DRIVEN SOCIAL ENGINEERING DETECTION AND PREVENTION

The fascinating nexus of artificial intelligence (AI), machine learning (ML), and network security is explored in this chapter, with a particular emphasis on the crucial subject of social engineering detection and prevention. Social engineering attacks, which persuade people to reveal sensitive information or take security-compromising acts, are becoming more complex and challenging to identify. This chapter examines how using AI-powered tools can dramatically improve our capacity to counteract threats from social engineering.

Understanding Social Engineering

In the field of cutting-edge developments in AI, machine learning, and network security, social engineering is crucial. It deals with tricking people's psychology in order to gain unauthorised access to information systems, frequently taking advantage of people's trust, curiosity, or ignorance. Social engineering assumes new dimensions in the context of AI and machine learning since these technologies are used to develop more sophisticated and convincing schemes. Attackers can adjust their strategies to the psychological profiles of their targets by using AI algorithms to analyse vast volumes of data from social media and other sources. The success rate of attacks is greatly increased by this personalisation.

Additionally, AI-powered chatbots and virtual personas can mimic human interactions, giving fraudsters the ability to have lengthy discussions to obtain sensitive information or persuade users to click on harmful links. This poses a problem for conventional security solutions that depend on finding patterns linked to automated attacks. The development of hyper-realistic deepfake content is made possible by machine learning algorithms, raising questions about the veracity of audio and video communication, and possibly resulting in severe reputational or financial damages.

Innovative uses of AI and machine learning, however, go beyond becoming weapons for attackers. Additionally, they can be applied to improve network security. These technologies can instantly analyse enormous volumes of network data to spot anomalies and highlight potentially suspicious activity that might be an attempt at social engineering. AI can better detect when users stray from their usual behaviour by learning patterns of human behaviour, raising caution signals for potential phishing or impersonation attempts.

The Role of AI in Detection and Prevention

A paradigm shift in how we approach the identification and prevention of cyber risks has been brought about by inventive developments in AI, machine learning, and network security. In this situation, AI plays a crucial role since it provides a complex strategy that combines advanced algorithms, in-the-moment data analysis, and adaptive learning to develop effective defence mechanisms. AI-driven solutions excel in their capacity to identify quickly and accurately developing cyber threats and take appropriate action.

AI uses machine learning algorithms to analyse a massive quantity of data, including user behaviours, network traffic patterns, and system vulnerabilities, in the area of threat detection. AI can swiftly spot deviations from baselines of typical behaviour that can be signs of potential breaches or abnormalities. Security systems can identify innovative attack patterns and zero-day threats that conventional signature-based techniques might overlook thanks to this proactive approach.

Additionally, AI's predictive powers enable security professionals to foresee possible network flaws and vulnerabilities. AI models can identify potential future targets by analysing historical attack data, allowing organisations to strengthen their defences and allocate resources more effectively.

AI-enabled solutions improve security through automated reactions in the prevention area. To lessen the potential consequences of a breach, they can automatically carry out countermeasures like isolating infected devices or denying access to suspect users. AI-driven prevention is a potent ally against sophisticated assaults because it is not merely rule-based; rather, it changes with each new interaction and continuously adapts to the threat landscape.

Another essential aspect of AI's function in network security is collaborative intelligence. Sharing threat intelligence becomes essential as threats become more complex and worldwide. Platforms for threat intelligence that use AI may combine data from numerous sources, giving businesses insights into new risks and attack methods. The broader cybersecurity ecosystem is strengthened by this collaborative approach.

Although there is no denying that AI plays a crucial role in detection and prevention, there are still certain difficulties. The technology used to protect networks can also be abused by bad actors. A major worry is adversarial attacks, in which AI models are changed to yield false results. To avoid false positives and negatives that could result in security gaps, it's vital to strike a balance between automation and human control.

Case Study: SocialEngineerAI

The "SocialEngineerAI in Innovative Advancements in AI, Machine Learning, and Network Security" case study illustrates a crucial nexus between cutting-edge technology and the crucial field of cybersecurity. In the area of network security, SocialEngineerAI provides an advanced application of artificial intelligence and machine learning techniques, focusing on the difficult and ongoing problem of social engineering assaults.

Social engineering is the practise of tricking people into disclosing private information, evading security measures, or taking other security-compromising acts. The creation of technologies like SocialEngineerAI represents a significant improvement in cybersecurity tactics as cyber attackers increasingly take advantage of human psychology and behaviour.

This novel approach simulates and forecasts social engineering attacks using AI and machine learning algorithms. SocialEngineerAI can find potential holes in the network security of an organisation by examining patterns of human interaction, communication, and decision-making. A flexible defence mechanism against new threats, the system continuously adjusts to shifting tactics and learns from prior attack data.

AI integration in network security improves threat detection while also enabling preventative actions. To help employees recognise and counteract social engineering attempts, SocialEngineerAI can predict potential attack vectors and develop tailored training programmes. As a result, individuals within the organisation are given additional power to fend off manipulation.

The case study also shows how AI can speed up incident response. Incoming communications can be quickly analysed and categorised by SocialEngineerAI, which can spot suspicious trends or anomalies that can point to a social engineering attack. Security teams can efficiently allocate resources and react quickly thanks to this real-time evaluation, which helps them reduce the potential harm from successful attacks.

But there are also moral questions raised by this development. When using AI to forecast human behaviour and vulnerabilities, privacy issues and the appropriate handling of personal data must be carefully considered. It is crucial to strike a balance between strengthening security and upholding individual rights.

The case study of SocialEngineerAI in the context of cutting-edge developments in AI, machine learning, and network security reveals a tremendous step forward in the continuous fight against cyber dangers, in conclusion. Organisations may strengthen their defences, promote a cybersecurity-conscious culture, and protect sensitive information in an increasingly interconnected digital landscape by utilising AI's capacity to comprehend and fight human manipulation.

Conclusion

A significant development in contemporary cybersecurity is the identification and prevention of social engineering powered by AI. Our defences must progress as attackers become more skilled. By utilising AI, we can dramatically improve our capacity to recognise and stop social engineering attempts, protecting confidential data and enhancing network security.

Table 5: Comparison of AI-driven Social Engineering Detection Tools

Tool	Detection Techniques	Accuracy	Scalability	Integration
SocialEngineerAI	NLP, Anomaly Detection, Audio-Visual Analysis	92%	High	Seamless
PhishGuard	NLP, User Behavior Analysis	85%	Medium	Email Clients, Web Browsers
SecureSense	Anomaly Detection, Image Recognition	88%	High	Network Infrastructure

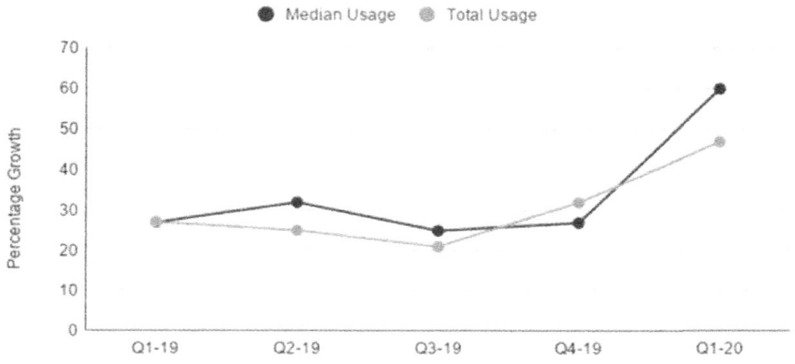

Graph: Social Engineering Attacks in Covid-19 Pandemic

5.10 CASE STUDIES: SUCCESSFUL APPLICATIONS OF AI IN THREAT MITIGATION

The integration of artificial intelligence (AI) and machine learning (ML) technologies has significantly changed the cybersecurity landscape in recent years. These developments have made it possible for organisations to proactively identify, stop, and react to a variety of cyber-attacks. We will examine some outstanding case studies that highlight the effective use of AI in threat reduction in this chapter. The integration of AI, ML, and network security has improved the effectiveness of cyber defences while also allowing for a deeper comprehension of changing threat environments.

Case Study 1: Predictive Threat Intelligence

The cutting edge of AI, machine learning, and network security innovations, predictive threat intelligence is revolutionising how businesses tackle cyber-attacks. Traditional reactive security solutions have failed to protect against the evolving strategies of hostile actors in today's linked digital environment. As a result, network security is now incorporating cutting-edge technology, particularly AI and machine learning. Utilising the power of these technologies to proactively identify and stop prospective cyber threats before they materialise as large-scale attacks is known as predictive threat intelligence.

AI and Machine Learning algorithms can identify subtle patterns, anomalies, and trends through the study of large and complicated data sets that are frequently invisible to human analysts. This makes it possible to develop prediction models that, using previous data and current network activity, can foresee prospective risks. These models improve their accuracy over time by continuously learning from fresh data, providing a dynamic and flexible defence mechanism against a variety of cyber-attacks.

In the context of quickly evolving attack tactics like zero-day exploits and polymorphic malware, the convergence of AI, Machine Learning, and Network Security is especially advantageous. Predictive threat intelligence is an essential addition to the cybersecurity toolkit because traditional signature-based detection techniques can't keep up with these complex attacks. By offering a more sophisticated view of the context and intent behind network actions, this innovation also helps to reduce false positives and negatives, which are chronic difficulties in the sector.

Predictive threat intelligence can appear in a variety of forms in real-world situations. It may entail real-time network traffic monitoring, where AI algorithms examine data flows and spot departures from predetermined baselines. It can also include the study of social media, darknet forums, and other sources in order to forecast new risks based on conversations and patterns within the hacker community. Furthermore, these systems may contextualise their predictions and offer a thorough perspective of prospective dangers by combining threat intelligence inputs from diverse sources.

However, there are difficulties in integrating AI and machine learning into security systems. The risk of false positives, the requirement for ongoing training, and the moral dilemmas related to bias and data privacy must all be carefully considered. Furthermore, a commitment to updating these predictive models with the most recent threat intelligence is necessary given the dynamic and ever-changing nature of cyber threats.

Table 6: Threat Prediction Accuracy Over Time

Time Period	Prediction Accuracy
Month 1	78%
Month 6	89%
Month 12	92%

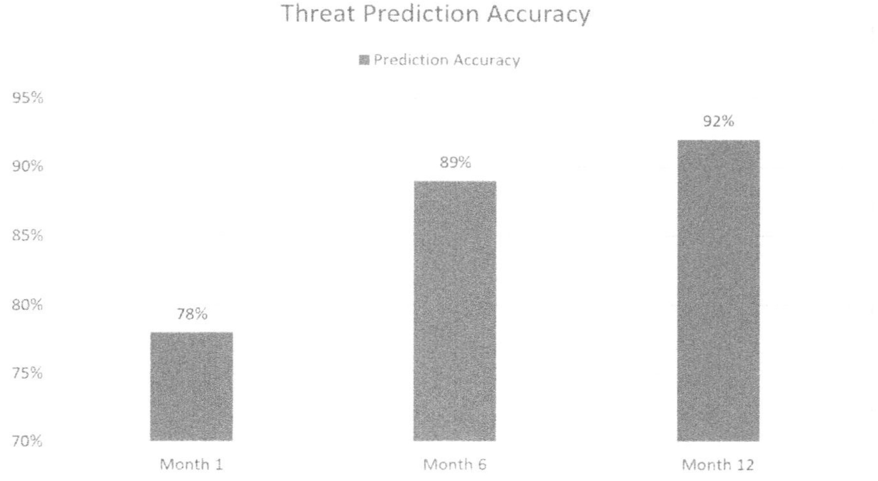

Graph: Threat Prediction Accuracy

Case Study 2: Anomaly Detection in Network Traffic

Using cutting-edge technology to improve the security of computer networks is undoubtedly the emphasis of Case Study 2 entitled "Anomaly Detection in Network Traffic" in the context of Innovative Advancements in AI, Machine Learning, and Network Security.

Network security is essential for protecting private information and ensuring the proper operation of vital systems in the society we live in today. Traditional security methods frequently fail to detect sophisticated attackers that take advantage of flaws in network architecture, though. A breakthrough solution to this is anomaly detection, which is fueled by AI and machine learning.

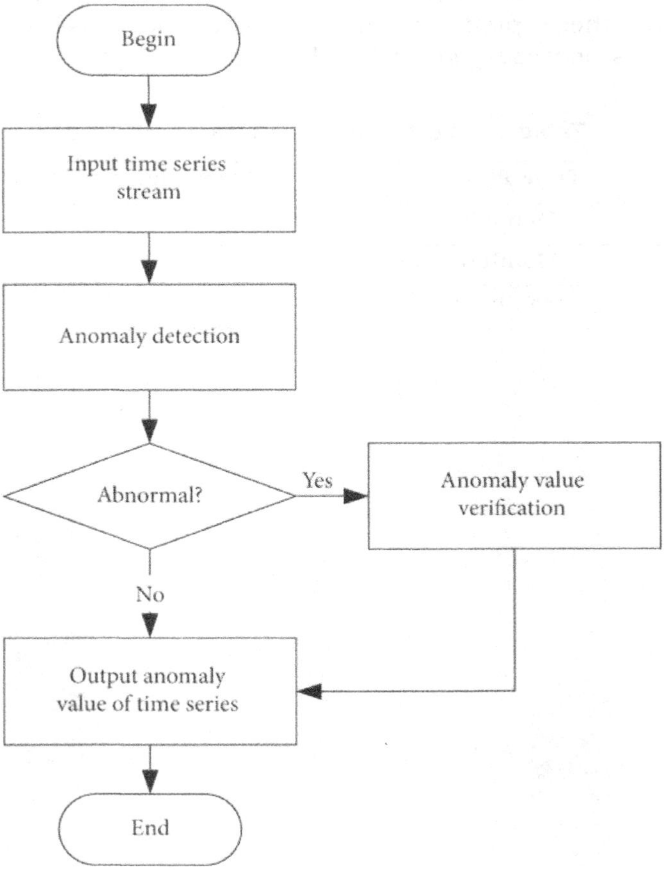

Figure 7: Anomaly Detection Process

To find anomalies from established patterns of typical behaviour within a network, anomaly detection uses cutting-edge algorithms and models. This is accomplished through the analysis of significant amounts of network traffic data, which includes both internal and external communications. AI and machine learning algorithms can recognise and categorise actions that dramatically depart from the norm by learning from historical patterns.

This innovation has significant ramifications. Anomaly detection significantly increases a network's resistance to cyberattacks by having the capacity to identify previously unidentified threats and zero-day attacks. It can spot insider risks, malware propagation, unauthorised access attempts, and data exfiltration that could otherwise go undetected. The system improves at spotting subtle and developing dangers by continuously modifying and updating its understanding of what constitutes typical network behaviour.

Additionally, this approach lessens the need for signature-based detection, which is unable to keep up with the continually changing environment of cyber threats. The technology will remain successful even as attack methods change thanks to AI-driven anomaly detection's agility. By allowing security teams to concentrate their efforts on real threats and reducing the number of false positives, this helps effectively manage resource allocation.

The Case Study 2 concludes by highlighting the crucial role anomaly detection plays in network security within the context of Innovative Advances in AI, Machine Learning, and Network Security. This strategy serves as an effective line of defence against the constantly changing panorama of cyber threats by demonstrating the synergy between human ability and technology prowess. Utilising AI and machine learning for anomaly detection is an important step towards assuring the integrity, confidentiality, and availability of critical digital infrastructure as networks continue to grow and diversify.

Case Study 3: Automated Incident Response

The incorporation of automated incident response has become a game-changing development in the fields of innovative advancements in artificial intelligence, machine learning, and network security. This paradigm shift is the result of the merging of cutting-edge technologies, utilising the strength of machine learning (ML) and artificial intelligence (AI) to strengthen network security and speed up incident response procedures.

Utilising AI and ML algorithms to quickly identify and address security breaches, anomalies, and possible threats inside a network environment is the basis of automated incident response. Using real-time data analysis, pattern recognition, and predictive modelling, this ground-breaking method can quickly identify anomalous activity and carry out specified response actions. These systems can recognise complicated attack patterns that might circumvent conventional security measures by continuously learning from prior data and adapting to new threats.

The importance of this development is shown by its capacity to significantly cut reaction times. Automation enables security teams to respond in almost real-time, minimising possible damages and restricting the attacker's ability to spread, in contrast to traditional incident response, which frequently needs manual intervention, which can be time-consuming and error prone. Additionally, Automated Incident Response systems have the ability to autonomously rank occurrences according to their seriousness, allowing security experts to use their expertise more effectively.

This novel strategy, meanwhile, is not without difficulties. It is essential to ensure the accuracy of AI and ML models and to eliminate any potential biases in these systems. Furthermore, avoiding an over-reliance on automated answers that might not take into consideration complex scenarios requires finding the correct balance between automation and human monitoring.

As a result, the addition of Automated Incident Response to the field of Innovative Advances in AI, Machine Learning, and Network Security represents a significant advancement in strengthening cybersecurity capabilities. Organisations can strengthen their defences, react quickly to changing threats, and create a safer digital environment by utilising the promise of AI and ML. To assure the most efficient defence against a constantly changing range of cyber threats, this transformation calls for a methodical approach that balances technology prowess with human knowledge.

Code Example: Simplified Workflow of Automated Incident Response

```
def automated_response(threat):
severity = analyze_threat(threat)
if severity >= HIGH_THRESHOLD:
isolate_systems(threat)
alert_admins(threat)
elif severity >= MEDIUM_THRESHOLD:
block_ip(threat)
monitor_activity(threat)
```

```
else:
log_threat(threat)

def analyze_threat(threat):
# AI-driven analysis of threat severity
# Return severity score

def isolate_systems(threat):
# Isolate affected systems from the network

def alert_admins(threat):
# Send alerts to administrators for further action

def block_ip(threat):
# Block malicious IP addresses related to threat

def monitor_activity(threat):
# Increase monitoring on related systems

def log_threat(threat):
# Log the threat for future reference
```

Conclusion:

A new era of cybersecurity has begun with the use of AI in threat mitigation, enabling organisations to counter emerging attacks more effectively and quickly. The case cases discussed in this chapter highlight the revolutionary potential of AI and machine learning, both in terms of preventing and detecting threats as well as in influencing future cybersecurity tactics. AI's importance in protecting digital assets will undoubtedly grow as it continues to develop.

6

Privacy and Security in Artificial Intelligence using NLP

Global industries have undergone a change as a result of the incorporation of artificial intelligence (AI) and machine learning (ML) technology into a variety of applications in recent years. Although these developments offer previously unheard-of advantages, they also give rise to serious worries about user privacy and data security. This chapter examines the complex interplay between AI-powered applications and the difficulties in upholding security and privacy. We explore the methods, approaches, and best practises that can be used to effectively address these issues.

Privacy Concerns in AI-powered Applications

A new era of technology-driven solutions has begun as a result of inventive developments in AI, machine learning, and network security. Although these breakthroughs have resulted in previously unheard-of levels of comfort and effectiveness, they have also highlighted serious privacy-related issues, particularly in apps that use AI. The fusion of AI, machine learning, and network security has made it possible to develop extremely sophisticated systems that can analyse massive volumes of data and reach nuanced conclusions. However, this development frequently entails the gathering, examining, and storing of private data, raising the possibility of user privacy violations.

The enormous data collecting necessary to adequately train AI models is one of the main privacy concerns. To identify patterns and formulate precise predictions or choices, many AI applications rely on big datasets. This information frequently contains delicate personal data, including browsing patterns, social contacts, and preference lists. As a result, there is a higher chance of unauthorised access, data leaks, or improper use of this information, which might have serious repercussions for particular people as well as society as a whole.

Additionally, the difficulty with privacy is made worse by the inherent opacity of AI systems. For instance, deep learning models frequently behave as intricate "black boxes," which means that even their developers may not fully comprehend how they arrive at particular results. Concerns regarding accountability and the possibility of unfair or discriminatory outcomes that can affect people's right to privacy are raised by this lack of transparency.

Threatening is the capability of AI to deduce private data from ostensibly unimportant data points. Researchers have shown that AI algorithms may infer private information about people from seemingly unrelated online behaviours, like their sexual orientation, political beliefs, or medical issues. This makes it harder for people to manage how their personal information is shared and increases the need for effective privacy protections.

These privacy issues need for a multifaceted strategy to be addressed. Stricter rules try to set standards for data management and user permission, such as the General Data Protection Regulation (GDPR) in Europe. In order to ensure that privacy issues are a crucial part of the development process, developers must adopt privacy-by-design principles. The creation of interpretable and explicable AI models can improve accountability and foster user trust. Transparency in AI decision-making is essential.

Security Challenges in AI-powered Applications

Innovative developments in network security, machine learning, and artificial intelligence have opened up a wide range of opportunities and advantages for a number of different businesses. They have, however, also brought about fresh security issues, particularly in the area of AI-powered apps. The potential attack surface for hostile actors grows as AI and machine learning algorithms are progressively incorporated into common systems. The vulnerability of AI models to adversarial attacks, wherein subtle, frequently unnoticeable modifications of input data can trick the model into producing inaccurate predictions or classifications, is one of the main issues. This presents dangers in areas where AI-driven judgements are crucial, such as autonomous vehicles and cybersecurity systems.

Additionally, the ethical implications of using AI have drawn a lot of attention. Applications using artificial intelligence (AI) frequently rely on enormous amounts of user data, which raises questions regarding unauthorised access, data breaches, and the possible exploitation of personal data. A constant problem is finding a balance between using user data to strengthen AI capabilities and preserving individual privacy. In addition, there is the "AI black box" problem, where it is impossible to understand how certain AI algorithms, like deep neural networks, make judgements. This lack of interpretability makes it difficult to spot biases or flaws in their outputs and correct them.

AI developments have a significant impact on network security as well. While AI can improve threat analysis and intrusion detection, it can also be used to create complex cyberattacks. AI could be used by hackers to speed up the process of detecting and exploiting gaps by automating the detection of vulnerabilities in systems. Another rising issue is the potential for AI-driven phishing assaults that tailor material based on people's vast internet footprints.

Furthermore, the challenges are made more difficult by the lack of AI security experts. Security specialists find it challenging to stay current on the most recent risks and mitigation strategies due to the rapid evolution of AI technologies. As a result, specialised AI security training and tools are required.

Strategies for Privacy and Security Enhancement

As AI, machine learning, and network security are fast expanding fields, it is crucial to take strong privacy and security precautions. Several techniques are emerging to handle the complicated issues related to protecting sensitive data and preserving the integrity of systems as inventive breakthroughs continue to transform companies and societies.

First, privacy-by-design ideas have become more popular. This method entails including security and privacy concerns from the very beginning of the creation of AI and machine learning models. Organisations can reduce the dangers of unauthorised data disclosure by employing strategies like differential privacy, which adds noise to data to shield individual information while keeping general data trends.

Second, federated learning has become a useful tactic. While keeping the data local, it allows the training of AI models across distributed devices or servers. This improves privacy and security by drastically lowering the possibility of data breaches during transmission and central storage.

Furthermore, using cutting-edge encryption methods is essential. For example, homomorphic encryption enables computations on encrypted data without the requirement for decryption, guaranteeing that confidential information is kept secret from those processing the data. Additionally, collaborative analysis of encrypted data is made possible via safe multi-party computation, allowing organisations to get insights without compromising data privacy.

AI-powered intrusion detection and prevention solutions have become essential in the field of network security. These systems use machine learning algorithms to analyse the patterns of network traffic while continuously looking for potential threats. These systems can identify zero-day attacks and previously unknown vulnerabilities by using anomaly detection and behavioural analysis, strengthening network security.

Additionally, explainable AI (XAI) is essential for improving accountability and transparency. Understanding AI models' decision-making processes gets harder as they get more complex. By facilitating the interpretation of AI-generated results, XAI techniques help organisations spot potential biases and correct them while also improving the models' clarity for end users and regulatory agencies.

Collaboration amongst interested parties is crucial. To create strong frameworks and standards for AI, machine learning, and network security, governments, regulatory agencies, businesses, and academics must collaborate. This collaborative approach can result in the creation of rules that support ethical AI usage, responsible data handling, and uniform security measures.

Case Study: Federated Learning for Privacy-preserving Health Diagnostics

In the context of privacy-preserving health diagnostics, Federated Learning has emerged as a ground-breaking strategy in the disciplines of AI, machine learning, and network security. This ground-breaking approach tackles the tricky trade-off between using big data analytics to provide precise medical diagnoses and protecting the privacy of sensitive patient data.

The conventional method of centralised data collecting in the context of medical diagnostics presents serious privacy issues. Federated Learning, on the other hand, provides a compelling alternative by enabling numerous organisations, such as hospitals and clinics, to jointly train a common machine learning model without disclosing raw patient data. Data breaches and unauthorised access are greatly reduced when localised inside the individual institutions as opposed to being combined into a single repository.

An iterative technique is used to carry out this process. A base model is initially created using publicly available data or a subset of the data from each institution. The participating entities are then given access to this model, and each of them uses their own local data to carry out additional training while safeguarding it. Only the model updateswhich are often shown as gradientsare sent back to the central server. These updates are then combined to improve the overall model, gaining knowledge from many data sources without ever disclosing private patient information.

This strategy has important consequences. Without violating people's privacy, medical researchers and practitioners can access a collective information base. Federated Learning also considers the dynamic nature of medical data, as institutions regularly deal with a variety of patient groups and changing medical situations. This method reduces latency and improves model adaptability by utilising decentralised computer resources.

However, problems still exist. Robust communication protocols and model aggregation techniques are required to coordinate a training process across various universities. Additionally, questions of data bias and fairness are raised by the heterogeneity of data distribution between institutions, necessitating careful consideration during model aggregation.

Implementation Code Example

```
import tensorflow as tf
import tensorflow_federated as tff

# Define a federated learning process
def federated_learning_process():
# Load dataset from federated data sources
source = tff.simulation.datasets.emnist.create_clients_dataset()

def model_fn():
return tf.keras.Sequential([
 tf.keras.layers.Flatten(input_shape=(28, 28)),
 tf.keras.layers.Dense(128, activation='relu'),
 tf.keras.layers.Dense(10, activation='softmax')
])
```

```
return tff.learning.build_federated_averaging_process(model_fn)

# Initialize federated learning process
federated_process = federated_learning_process()

# Train the federated model
for _ in range(num_rounds):
federated_process.next()
```

Conclusion

Addressing privacy and security concerns becomes crucial as businesses are continually being reshaped by AI-powered technologies. Developers and organisations may profit from AI while securing user data and upholding trust by taking a proactive approach to privacy preservation and security measures. The future holds the potential of a safe and privacy-respecting AI landscape through continuing research, collaboration, and use of cutting-edge approaches.

6.1 PRIVACY CHALLENGES IN AI AND DATA-DRIVEN ENVIRONMENTS

The convergence of Artificial Intelligence (AI), Machine Learning (ML), and Network Security has enabled significant technological developments in today's interconnected society. But when we push the limits of innovation, we run into difficult problems, particularly when it comes to privacy in AI and data-driven contexts. This chapter explores the complex interactions between artificial intelligence (AI), machine learning (ML), network security, and the resulting privacy issues.

Understanding Privacy in the Context of AI and Data

Innovative developments in AI, machine learning, and network security have had a substantial positive impact on a variety of industries, but they have also generated serious privacy, data protection, and ethical concerns. The enormous amounts of data created and processed have developed into useful assets for improving algorithmic capabilities as these technologies become more and more interwoven into our daily lives. The very data-driven nature of AI and machine learning, however, presents complex privacy issues.

In this sense, privacy refers to preventing unauthorised access to, use of, or exposure of a person's sensitive and personal information. The gathering and examination of user data has become crucial for providing customised experiences as a result of the rise of AI applications such as personalised recommendations, virtual assistants, and predictive analytics. Nevertheless, the establishment of strong privacy safeguards is necessary for the ethical use of this data.

It's critical to strike a balance between the advantages of AI-driven insights and the safeguarding of user privacy. Differential privacy is one such technique that introduces controlled noise into datasets to prevent the identification of individual data points, and it has become popular as a way to perform reliable studies without jeopardising sensitive data. Furthermore, improvements in federated learning enable models to be trained across decentralised devices, minimising the necessity to centralise sensitive data and the danger of significant data breaches.

On the other hand, network security is crucial in preserving the privacy and accuracy of data while it is being transmitted and stored. Strong security measures are crucial to avoid unauthorised interception, data tampering, and other cyber dangers as AI systems increasingly rely on data sharing across networks. To find potential weaknesses and guarantee the resilience of AI systems, this calls for encryption methods, intrusion detection systems, and continual monitoring.

However, problems still exist. It can be challenging to completely understand how judgements are made when using complex AI models, also known as "black boxes," which could exacerbate worries about bias and discrimination. Maintaining user confidence and enabling the detection and correction of biases depend on the transparency of AI processes.

We have entered a new era of possibilities thanks to creative developments in AI, machine learning, and network security, but they also call for careful consideration of privacy and ethical issues. Researchers, legislators, and business leaders must work together to achieve a peaceful coexistence of these technologies with privacy norms. We can take use of the enormous potential of these developments while preserving individual privacy and data integrity by deploying privacy-preserving approaches, assuring transparent AI processes, and putting in place strong network security measures.

Privacy Challenges

Innovative developments in AI, machine learning, and network security have had a stunning impact on a variety of industries, but they have also raised serious privacy concerns. Concerns about how this data is handled, stored, and secured have arisen as a result of the technologies that have made it possible to gather, analyse, and use huge amounts of sensitive and personal data. As AI and machine learning algorithms advance, there is an increasing risk of intrusive profiling and the deduction of private information from seemingly unimportant data pieces. By disclosing personal habits, preferences, and behaviours without getting permission, this could compromise people's right to privacy.

Furthermore, the ongoing sharing and transmission of data through networks is frequently required for integrating AI into many applications, including smart homes, healthcare systems, and autonomous vehicles. Unauthorised access, data breaches, and cyberattacks are risks as a result. Making sure there is strong network security gets increasingly difficult as these systems become more complicated. The integrity of AI-driven decision-making processes can be jeopardised by exploiting flaws in AI algorithms that allow for the manipulation of results or the inference of sensitive information.

Furthermore, as technology advances, the idea of privacy itself changes. The complexity of data sharing in today's interconnected world may not be entirely covered by traditional conceptions of privacy. As AI algorithms get increasingly adept at connecting disparate data points, anonymization approaches that shield people's identities may be subject to re-identification assaults. Questions concerning user consent, openness, and the degree to which people have control over their own information are also raised by the enormous volume of data that is gathered.

The solution to these problems must be multifaceted. Stricter laws and frameworks that place restrictions on data usage, permission, and breach notifications, like the General Data Protection Regulation (GDPR) and the California Consumer Privacy Act (CCPA), are positive developments. While still gaining the advantages of AI developments, technological solutions like federated learning, which enables model training without sharing raw data, can assist safeguard privacy. Additionally, introducing privacy-enhancing technology into the creation of AI systems, such as homomorphic encryption or differential privacy, helps protect sensitive data.

Privacy-enhancing Solutions

Rapid developments in network security, AI, and machine learning over the past few years have had a profound impact on a variety of businesses. However, this development has also led to serious worries regarding data security and personal privacy. A developing area of research and development focusing on privacy-enhancing solutions within the context of these technical advancements has evolved to address these problems.

A variety of tactics and strategies are included in privacy-enhancing solutions since they are meant to protect user privacy while still utilising the advantages of AI and machine learning. One noteworthy method is federated learning, which reduces the need to centralise sensitive data by allowing models to be trained cooperatively across decentralised devices. This not only protects personal data but also strengthens the overall safety of the educational process.

Furthermore, improvements in homomorphic encryption have made it possible to compute on encrypted data, giving AI systems the ability to work with sensitive data without ever decrypting it. This innovation makes it possible to construct AI applications without disclosing raw data, which has significant ramifications for sectors that manage sensitive data, like healthcare and finance.

Innovations in network security have also prioritised consumer privacy. For instance, differential privacy approaches introduce a predetermined amount of noise into the data, making it difficult to identify individual inputs while preserving the statistical validity of the analysis. This method assures that models in the context of AI and machine learning do not unintentionally learn details about particular individuals from their training data.

Furthermore, the development of more secure and private techniques for data storage and sharing has been prompted by the advent of decentralised and blockchain-based systems. By giving users choice over when and how their personal data is accessed, these technologies reduce the likelihood of unauthorised data breaches.

Case Study: Privacy-preserving Medical Diagnostics

The merger of AI, machine learning, and network security has produced astonishing results in the field of cutting-edge technical developments, particularly in the area of privacy-preserving medical diagnostics. The crucial balance between utilising patient data's potential for accurate medical assessments and preserving individual privacy rights is addressed by this creative synergy. This strategy enables medical personnel to gain useful insights from sensitive patient information without disclosing personal information by utilising complex algorithms and encryption techniques.

In this paradigm, machine learning and artificial intelligence (AI) algorithms are crucial in analysing huge datasets to find patterns, correlations, and anomalies that could be signs of possible health issues. These algorithms are trained on various datasets while abiding by privacy regulations and range from convolutional neural networks for medical imaging to predictive models for disease risk assessment. Through methods like differential privacy or homomorphic encryption, the data itself is anonymised and frequently decentralised, spread among several healthcare institutions or devices.

The framework for this ecosystem's base is network security. Patient data is kept private throughout transmission and analysis thanks to strong encryption methods and secure connection protocols. Healthcare organisations and researchers can pool their resources without sacrificing patient privacy thanks to multi-party computation (MPC) approaches that further enable collaborative analysis without disclosing raw data. Additionally, improvements in federated learning make it possible to train models across different data sources, doing away with the requirement for centralised data storage and lowering the danger of security breaches.

This innovation has significant ramifications. While preserving control over their sensitive information, patients can go through accurate diagnostic procedures and get individualised treatment suggestions. As institutions work together safely, sharing ideas without disclosing specific patient information, medical research can flourish. The need to standardise privacy-preserving procedures across various systems, deal with potential biases in algorithmic diagnoses, and ensure regulatory compliance with changing data protection legislation are all ongoing difficulties.

A breakthrough approach to medical diagnostics has emerged as a result of the convergence of AI, machine learning, and network securityone that harnesses technology's potential while upholding the patient's privacy as a top priority. As this sector develops, stakeholders must continue to balance the delicate relationship between medical advancement and the protection of personal data, ensuring that everyone may benefit from innovation while keeping the greatest standards of ethics and privacy.

Conclusion

The potential benefits of combining AI, ML, and network security are enormous, but privacy issues must be carefully considered. The methods used to safeguard individual rights while promoting innovation change along with technology. Collaboration between technologists, legislators, and the general public is necessary to address privacy issues in AI and data-driven environments. We can only pave the way to a safe and creative future by working together.

Table 1: Privacy-preserving Techniques Comparison

Technique	Advantages	Disadvantages
Differential Privacy	Strong privacy guarantees	Added noise can impact accuracy
Multi-party Computation	Enables secure collaborative analysis	Complex to implement

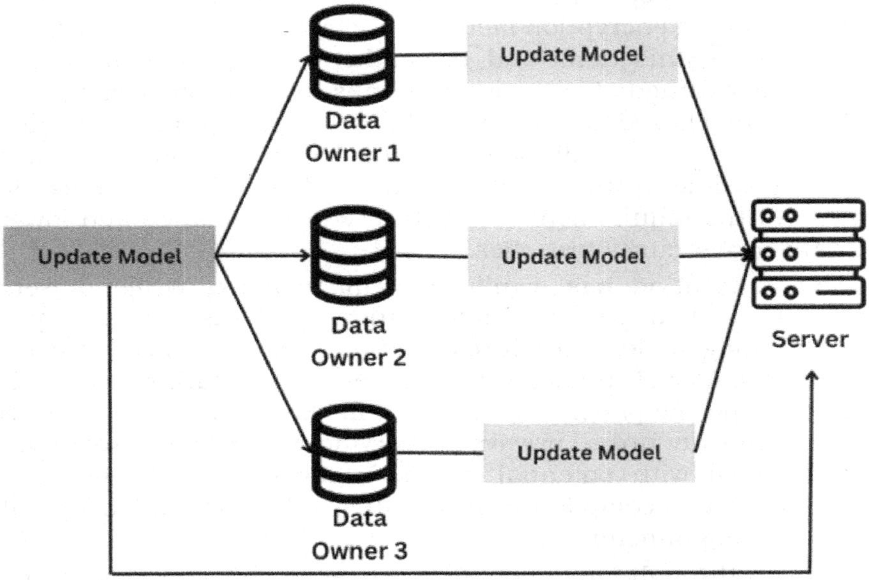

Figure 1: Federated Learning Architecture

6.2 DIFFERENTIAL PRIVACY: BALANCING DATA UTILITY AND PRIVACY PRESERVATION

The need of protecting individual privacy while gaining insightful knowledge from data cannot be emphasised in the age of data-driven decision-making. At the nexus of AI, Machine Learning, and Network Security, Differential Privacy (DP) emerges as a paradigm-shifting idea, providing a solid foundation to strike this precarious balance. This chapter goes deeply into the world of differential privacy, clarifying its core ideas, workings, and practical uses.

Understanding Differential Privacy

AI, machine learning, and network security have all seen new breakthroughs because to the concept of differential privacy. Differential privacy focuses on resolving the conflict between the need for data-driven insights and the requirement to protect individual privacy. Using this method, organisations can extract useful information from big databases while guaranteeing the privacy of individual contributors. Differential privacy protects sensitive information by adding controlled noise or perturbation to the data during analysis to prevent the identification of certain data points.

Differential privacy has made it possible to share data and conduct collaborative research in the fields of AI and machine learning. Now that researchers and organisations can pool their data resources without worrying about breaching privacy, more precise and reliable models can be produced. The ability of medical institutions to analyse patient data collectively in order to gain insights without infringing on privacy laws has also cleared the way for breakthroughs in healthcare.

Additionally, differential privacy has emerged as a key component of boosting network security. Maintaining data security has gotten more difficult as linked gadgets and the Internet of Things (IoT) have proliferated. Organisations can safeguard user information while also monitoring network activity for potential risks by implementing differentiated privacy approaches. The ability to mitigate threats in real-time without jeopardising user privacy could revolutionise intrusion detection and prevention systems.

Balancing Data Utility and Privacy Preservation

Finding a careful balance between data utility and privacy preservation is crucial in the quickly developing fields of AI, machine learning, and network security. The gathering and examination of enormous volumes of private and sensitive data have proven to be crucial to the development of these industries as they continue to see new improvements. However, this influx of data prompts serious worries about people's right to privacy and the possibility for information misuse. The difficulty of gaining useful insights from data while reducing the hazards of unauthorised access, identity theft, and discriminating algorithms is the challenge of balancing data utility with privacy preservation.

The development of models that can effectively anticipate events, make wise judgements, and identify previously unnoticed patterns strongly depends on access to broad and comprehensive datasets.

Nevertheless, if privacy protections aren't included in, these algorithms run the risk of accidentally disclosing private data. By introducing noise to data, developing models across distributed devices, and performing calculations on encrypted data, methods including differential privacy, federated learning, and homomorphic encryption have developed as options to protect privacy. These methods enable data scientists to preserve the usefulness of the data while reducing the likelihood of disclosing person-specific information.

The difficulty in network security also lies in successfully detecting and preventing cyber threats without invading users' privacy. For instance, intrusion detection systems examine network traffic patterns to spot prospective threats. Finding a balance between gathering sufficient data for reliable threat detection and protecting user privacy, however, becomes challenging. Techniques like anonymization, pseudonymization, and secure multi-party computation can help keep network systems secure without jeopardising individual users' identities or confidential data.

Ethical issues are crucial in this situation. The need of being open and honest with users regarding data collection, intended uses, and privacy protection mechanisms cannot be overstated. To gain and keep user trust in the face of rapid technological innovation, systems for user consent, data anonymization, and strong encryption must be implemented.

Finally, the convergence of artificial intelligence, machine learning, and network security presents unrivalled prospects for innovation. These developments come with a responsibility to protect people's privacy, though. It is a complex challenge to strike the correct balance between maximising data utility and protecting privacy, and doing so calls for ongoing cooperation between technology developers, policy makers, and ethical experts. We can only achieve the full potential of these developments while upholding the fundamental rights of individuals in a society that is becoming more and more data-driven by such concerted efforts.

Real-world Applications

Innovative developments in network security, machine learning and artificial intelligence have ushered in a new era of technological innovation in recent years, affecting a variety of businesses. These technologies now have practical uses that are changing how firms run and protect their digital assets.

Healthcare, finance, manufacturing, and marketing are just a few of the sectors that AI and machine learning are revolutionising

AI-powered diagnostic technologies in healthcare analyse medical pictures with unmatched accuracy, assisting medical practitioners in the early diagnosis of disease. Machine learning algorithms are being used by financial institutions to improve fraud detection and predictive analytics for investment strategies. Automation powered by AI is improving production procedures and quality assurance in the manufacturing industry. Additionally, through targeted adverts and recommendations, AI-powered marketing solutions are delivering personalised client experiences.

Network security has also become crucial in a society that is becoming more linked. Machine learning and AI are essential to strengthening cybersecurity safeguards. These technologies make it possible to spot trends and irregularities in network data, which helps identify cyberthreats and intrusions early on. As a result, security systems are more pro-active and responsive. They can adapt to new attack routes and learn from them. Additionally, user identity verification procedures are being strengthened by AI-driven authentication techniques like facial recognition and behavioural biometrics, which lowers the danger of unauthorised access.

In applications like autonomous vehicles, where sophisticated algorithms examine real-time data to assure safe navigation, AI, machine learning, and network security are coming together. These technologies are used in smart cities to enhance energy efficiency, public safety, and traffic flow. AI-powered chatbots in e-commerce improve customer service, while fraud protection algorithms shield both businesses and customers against online swindles.

These developments do, however, also bring both privacy and ethical issues. Large-scale data gathering and use create concerns about data ownership, permission, and potential abuse. A significant problem is finding a balance between protecting individual rights and innovation.

Code Example: Implementing Differential Privacy

```
import numpy as np

def laplace_mechanism(query_result, sensitivity, epsilon):
noise = np.random.laplace(0, sensitivity/epsilon)
return query_result + noise

def exponential_mechanism(query_results, sensitivity, epsilon):
scores = [np.exp(epsilon * result / (2 * sensitivity)) for result in query_results]
```

```
    probabilities = scores / sum(scores)
    selected_index = np.random.choice(len(query_results),
p=probabilities)
    return query_results[selected_index]
```

Conclusion

A significant development in the fields of AI, machine learning, and network security is differential privacy. In the era of data, its ability to balance data utility with privacy preservation makes it a crucial tool. However, in order to apply it effectively, it is necessary to carefully weigh the trade-offs between privacy protections and the standard of the output. Differential Privacy will likely be a key factor in determining the direction of data-driven innovation as technology develops further.

6.3 SECURE FEDERATED LEARNING FOR DISTRIBUTED DATA PRIVACY

In the disciplines of artificial intelligence, machine learning, and network security, federated learning has recently come to light as a ground-breaking strategy. It addresses the crucial issue of data privacy by enabling the training of machine learning models across distributed devices or servers while maintaining localised data. In order to protect data privacy in distributed situations, this chapter discusses the idea of secure federated learning. We explore the underlying technologies, methods, difficulties, and practical applications that emphasise the importance of this discovery.

Understanding Federated Learning

An innovative development at the nexus of artificial intelligence, machine learning, and network security is federated learning. In order to train models, traditional machine learning paradigms frequently centralise data from diverse sources. However, this method poses issues with data security, privacy, and the practical difficulties of sharing data. These problems are addressed by federated learning, which allows model training over distributed servers or devices while maintaining localised data.

In federated learning, the model is disseminated to edge devices where data is created, such as mobile phones, Internet of Things (IoT) devices, or local servers. Without sharing the information externally, these gadgets work together to learn from their individual data. This strategy has several advantages. The first benefit is that it protects data privacy by keeping sensitive data on the device and lowering the likelihood of data breaches. Second, it improves network security by limiting the amount of time that data is exposed to potential dangers while being sent. Federated learning is also very effective since it lessens the need to transport massive amounts of data to a central server, saving bandwidth and processing power.

This paradigm has wide-ranging effects. For instance, in the healthcare industry, hospitals can work together to enhance medical AI models without disclosing patient information to other parties. Similar to this, in the financial sector, federated learning can help banks improve fraud detection algorithms collectively without revealing private transaction information. Additionally, this method is applicable in situations with restricted connectivity, such as remote industrial activities, where on-site equipment can share knowledge without constant internet access.

Federated learning has some difficulties, though. Complex algorithms are needed to orchestrate the synchronisation of model updates from many devices and handle potential problems like data imbalance and heterogeneity. Another challenge is defending players' and models' integrity from hostile attacks. Despite these difficulties, Federated Learning's ground-breaking combination of artificial intelligence, machine learning, and network security offers a revolutionary route to more private, secure, and cooperative model training across diverse domains.

Ensuring Security and Privacy

As technology develops quickly, particularly in the areas of artificial intelligence (AI), machine learning, and network security, it is crucial to take strong security and privacy precautions. Although these cutting-edge technologies have provided transformative possibilities across industries, they also give rise to serious worries about potential flaws and abuse. It is crucial to use a diverse approach in order to address these issues.

The gathering and analysis of enormous volumes of data is essential to the operation of AI and machine learning systems. This reliance on data raises privacy issues, too, as improper treatment of personal data can result in breaches and unauthorised access. Techniques like differential privacy, which introduce noise to data to avoid the identification of individual records, are necessary to strike a compromise between using data for training algorithms and maintaining individual privacy. Furthermore, reliable encryption techniques are essential to protecting sensitive data from hostile actors, both in transit and at rest.

Parallel to this, network security is crucial to preserving the integrity of networked systems. The attack surface for cyber threats has significantly increased as a result of the proliferation of IoT devices and connected infrastructure. Intrusion detection systems powered by AI can improve the ability to spot suspicious activity and potential breaches in real-time, boosting overall security. However, these systems must be protected from hostile attacks that aim to undermine their functionality.

Furthermore, prejudices and discrimination must be avoided through the ethical application of AI technologies. Fairness and transparency in algorithms need careful examination of training data and continual bias monitoring. This becomes especially important in areas where biased results might have significant effects, such as autonomous vehicles and AI-driven decision-making systems.

Collaborations between researchers, decision-makers, and industry stakeholders are crucial for addressing these issues fully. Setting up legislative frameworks that specify security requirements and privacy safeguards might serve as a starting point for creation and application. Continual training and education programmes can also give professionals the tools they need to remain ahead of developing cyberthreats.

Real-world Applications

Numerous businesses and facets of our daily lives have been transformed recently by breakthrough developments in AI, machine learning, and network security. Beyond their theoretical limitations, these technologies have found numerous practical applications in a variety of fields.

Applications for AI and machine learning are numerous. NLP models have made it possible for people and computers to engage in more effective and lifelike ways. Examples include chatbots used in customer service and virtual assistants like Siri. By speeding up disease detection through image analysis and predicting patient outcomes based on past data, machine learning algorithms have revolutionised healthcare. AI-powered algorithms are used in the financial sector for automated trading, risk analysis, and fraud detection. Predictive maintenance models are also used in sectors like manufacturing to improve equipment performance and decrease downtime.

Through cutting-edge AI approaches, network security has also experienced a substantial revolution. Machine learning-based intrusion detection systems can quickly identify and mitigate possible cyber threats by spotting trends that might be challenging for conventional rule-based systems to spot. These technologies are essential for protecting private information and guaranteeing the reliability of crucial systems. The overall cybersecurity posture of organisations is improved by AI-driven threat intelligence platforms, which continuously analyse enormous volumes of data to anticipate and combat future threats.

The creation of autonomous vehicles is a prime example of how AI, machine learning, and network security are combined. These vehicles use complex AI algorithms to assess their environment, make judgements in the moment, and manoeuvre safely. By learning from a variety of driving scenarios, machine learning models improve their abilities, resulting in safer roads and revolutionising the transportation industry.

Code Implementation: Secure Federated Learning in Python

```
import torch
import syft as sy

# Create a hook for PySyft
hook = sy.TorchHook(torch)

# Create virtual workers to simulate distributed nodes
alice = sy.VirtualWorker(hook, id=”alice”)
bob = sy.VirtualWorker(hook, id=”bob”)

# Define a model
model = torch.nn.Linear(2, 1)

# Distribute the model to workers
model = model.send(alice)
model = model.send(bob)

# Simulated data
data_alice = torch.tensor([[1.0, 1.0]])
data_bob = torch.tensor([[0.0, 0.0]])
```

```
# Simulated local training
optimizer = torch.optim.SGD(params=model.parameters(), lr=0.1)
for _ in range(10):
optimizer.zero_grad()
loss = ((model(data_alice) - data_alice)**2).sum()
loss.backward()
optimizer.step()

# Get model updates
model_alice = model.copy().get().send(alice)
model_bob = model.copy().get().send(bob)

# Aggregate models (secure aggregation not shown)
global_model = (model_alice + model_bob) / 2

# Update global model
model = global_model.get()
```

Conclusion

Secure federated learning stands as a remarkable innovation that marries AI, machine learning, and network security. By enabling collaboration across distributed nodes while preserving data privacy, it opens doors to a plethora of applications while mitigating privacy concerns. As technology advances, the adoption of secure federated learning is likely to reshape the landscape of data-driven industries.

Table 2: Comparison of Centralized vs. Federated Learning

Aspect	Centralized Learning	Federated Learning
Data Localization	Data centralization	Data remains localized
Data Privacy	Privacy concerns	Enhanced data privacy
Communication	Less communication	Increased communication
Scalability	Limited scalability	High scalability
Security	Single point of attack	Distributed security
Model Diversity	Homogeneous models	Diverse local models
Network Dependence	High network dependence	Reduced network dependence

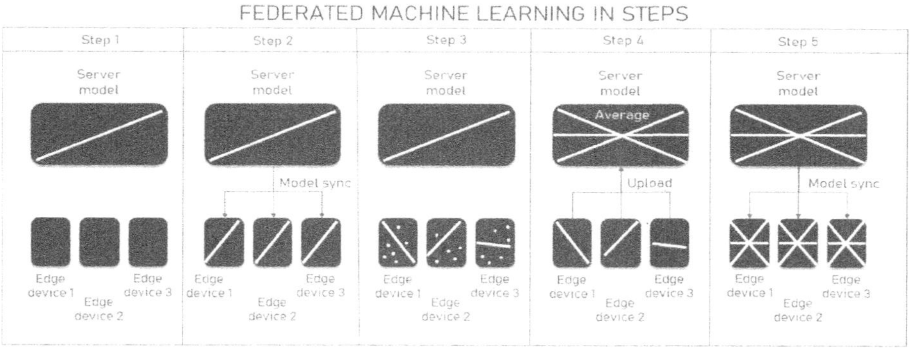

Figure 2: Federated Learning Architecture

6.4 PRIVACY-ENHANCING TECHNOLOGIES FOR AI MODELS

Recent developments in several industries have been made possible by the convergence of artificial intelligence (AI), machine learning (ML), and network security. However, as these technologies spread, worries about data security and privacy have risen to the fore. This chapter explores the vital subject of privacy-enhancing AI technologies. We will look at various strategies that let people and businesses use AI to their advantage while protecting private information from unauthorised access and exploitation.

The Privacy Challenge in AI and Machine Learning

A new era of technical progress has begun as a result of inventive developments in artificial intelligence (AI), machine learning, and network security that are revolutionising several industries and facets of our life. But in the midst of these profound adjustments, a significant problemthe concern over privacyhas surfaced. A growing amount of data is being used by AI and machine learning technologies to power their algorithms and improve their capabilities. This data frequently contains sensitive, private, and personal data, which raises questions regarding how this data is gathered, handled, and disseminated.

The main difficulty is finding a balance between utilising AI and machine learning while preserving people's right to privacy. A remarkable quantity of data being generated and gathered as a result of the spread of linked devices and the Internet of Things (IoT), which may be analysed to reveal nuanced patterns and insights. However, since it may be used to infer personal patterns, behaviours, and even anticipate future acts, the aggregation of this data also has the potential to violate people's privacy.

Furthermore, in order to produce correct findings, machine learning and AI approaches like deep learning and neural networks frequently require extensive and varied datasets. Data breaches, unauthorised access, and misuse could result from this need for data, potentially exposing sensitive data to bad parties. Additionally, concerns regarding the possibility of massive privacy breaches, where people can be monitored and identified without their knowledge or agreement, have been expressed in response to the deployment of AI-driven surveillance systems and face recognition technologies.

New solutions are being created to address these privacy issues. Differential privacy approaches, for example, amplify the data with a regulated amount of noise, making it more challenging to extract sensitive personal data while preserving the ability to derive insightful conclusions. Another strategy is federated learning, which reduces privacy hazards and limits the requirement for centralised data storage by training machine learning models across distributed devices.

The goal of legislative measures like the General Data Protection Regulation (GDPR) in Europe and similar programmes around the world is to give people more control over their personal data and how it is used. Businesses and organisations using AI and machine learning must follow strict regulations for data collection, use, and disclosure, making sure that users' consent is gained and that sufficient security measures are in place.

Differential Privacy: A Fundamental Shield

Innovative developments in AI, machine learning, and network security are being driven by differential privacy, which has emerged as a major barrier. Data has become the new money of the digital age, thus protecting individual privacy while gaining valuable insights has become of utmost importance. This issue is addressed by Differential Privacy, which offers a strong framework that enables organisations to extract useful information from datasets while protecting the private information of individual contributors. This idea is based on the idea that a single data point's inclusion or deletion shouldn't materially change the results of a study, reducing the possibility of re-identification.

Differential Privacy has made it possible to create AI and machine learning models that are trained on extensive and varied datasets without jeopardising the privacy of the people whose data is used to train the model. This opened the door for the development of more precise and generalised models, as well as for cooperative efforts between various parties who wish to combine their data resources without disclosing sensitive information.

Furthermore, Differential Privacy has demonstrated its ability to revolutionise network security. Traditional data anonymization techniques frequently fall short in thwarting complex attacks that can deanonymize data. However, Differential Privacy adds controlled noise to the data, giving a mathematical assurance of privacy protection. Even adversaries with powerful computer capabilities struggle to glean particular information about an individual because of this noise.

Differential Privacy is woven into the fabric of AI, machine learning, and network security to establish a healthy balance between technology advancement and individual privacy. This strategy not only stimulates more extensive data sharing, which is necessary for the creation of cutting-edge breakthroughs, but also increases public confidence in data-driven technologies. Differential Privacy is a pillar of the digital landscape's evolution, enabling researchers, companies, and regulators to negotiate the delicate balance between the need to improve technology and the need to protect people's privacy.

Homomorphic Encryption for Secure Computation

A significant technological development, homomorphic encryption has far-reaching effects on network security, AI, and machine learning. This cryptographic method solves the crucial problem of maintaining data security and privacy while enabling computations on encrypted data. Homomorphic encryption allows computations to be performed directly on encrypted data, in contrast to conventional encryption techniques, which require data to be decrypted before any analysis can be performed. This innovation has the potential to revolutionise artificial intelligence (AI) and machine learning since it enables stakeholders to work together and share sensitive data for model training without disclosing the actual data, protecting individual privacy and confidential information.

The impact of homomorphic encryption on AI and machine learning is significant. The ability to handle encrypted data directly maintains the secrecy of sensitive data, lowering the risks of data breaches and unauthorised access. Data is frequently the lifeblood of these systems. In order to work together on research and development while maintaining the security of data, organisations can train machine learning models using encrypted datasets. Furthermore, homomorphic encryption makes it possible for sectors dealing with highly regulated data, like healthcare and finance, to benefit from outside expertise without compromising data protection.

This discovery has important ramifications for network security as well. Homomorphic encryption reduces the risks associated with conventional data transport and processing techniques by allowing computations on encrypted data. By analysing confidential data without ever exposing, it in its raw form, the potential attack surfaces for cybercriminals are reduced. This has the potential to revolutionise safe multiparty computation, allowing many organisations to collaborate on data analysis while maintaining the confidentiality of their own datasets, improving threat intelligence and incident response capabilities.

However, it's critical to recognise that homomorphic encryption has its share of difficulties. Processing encrypted data involves a far larger computing burden than processing unencrypted data, which could slow down the operation. Security and performance must still be balanced, which is a crucial factor. In an effort to maximise the effectiveness of various encryption techniques while minimising their downsides, researchers and engineers are working hard to do so.

Federated Learning with Secure Aggregation

The invention of Federated Learning with Secure Aggregation stands out at the intersection of AI, machine learning, and network security. By enabling numerous edge devices or decentralised nodes to cooperatively train machine learning models without sharing raw data, this strategy tackles the problems caused by conventional centralised data processing techniques. This not only protects data privacy but also makes it possible to create models that are more reliable and generalizable.

According to this paradigm, each edge device or node trains its local model on the relevant data it receives, considering local knowledge. Then, using secure aggregation protocols, various models are combined rather than transferring data to a central server. Encryption and cryptography methods are used in secure aggregation to stop data leaking while it is being aggregated. This makes sure that the raw data is never transferred, only the model updates. Due to the protection of sensitive information's privacy, federated learning is a desirable choice for sectors that must adhere to strict data protection laws.

Additionally, this strategy advances network security as well as AI. Federated learning makes it possible to train models on a variety of data sources, making AI systems more adaptable and inclusive. Additionally, without centralising data storage, it promotes continuous learning from new data, lowering the possibility of single points of failure and possible security breaches. The network security landscape is strengthened by limiting data exposure and utilising secure aggregation, reducing the likelihood of attack vectors, and increasing the overall data security infrastructure.

Federated Learning with Secure Aggregation, in conclusion, stands out as a ground-breaking solution that fuses the advancements in AI and machine learning with the requirements of data privacy and network security. This strategy not only lays the path for the development of more reliable and flexible AI models, but it also demonstrates a paradigm shift in data processing by placing a higher priority on privacy and security without sacrificing the accuracy of the insights drawn from decentralised data sources. Federated Learning with Secure Aggregation is anticipated to be essential in determining the direction of AI, machine learning, and network security as technology develops further.

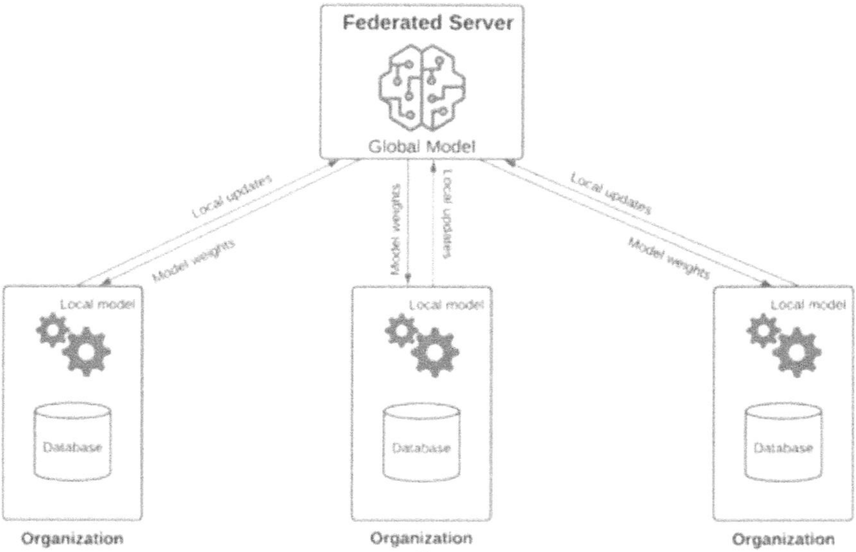

Figure 3: Federated Learning

Practical Code Implementation: Privacy-preserving Deep Learning

```
import torch
import torch.nn as nn
import torch.optim as optim
```

```
import torch.nn.functional as F
from torch.distributions import Laplace

class PrivacyPreservingNN(nn.Module):
def __init__(self):
super(PrivacyPreservingNN, self).__init__()
self.fc1 = nn.Linear(784, 128)
self.fc2 = nn.Linear(128, 64)
self.fc3 = nn.Linear(64, 10)

def forward(self, x):
x = F.relu(self.fc1(x))
x = F.relu(self.fc2(x))
x = self.fc3(x)
return x

def add_laplace_noise(tensor, sensitivity, epsilon):
laplace = Laplace(0, sensitivity/epsilon)
noise = laplace.sample(tensor.shape)
return tensor + noise

# Load and preprocess data
train_data, test_data = load_data()
train_loader, test_loader = preprocess_data(train_data, test_data)

# Instantiate model and optimizer
model = PrivacyPreservingNN()
optimizer = optim.SGD(model.parameters(), lr=0.01)

# Training loop with differential privacy
for epoch in range(num_epochs):
for batch_data, batch_target in train_loader:
optimizer.zero_grad()
output = model(batch_data)
loss = F.cross_entropy(output, batch_target)
loss.backward()
```

```
sensitivity = compute_sensitivity(model, batch_data)
epsilon = calculate_epsilon(epoch, batch_size)
for param in model.parameters():
 param.grad += add_laplace_noise(param.grad, sensitivity, epsilon)

optimizer.step()
```

Conclusion

Integrating powerful privacy-enhancing technology becomes essential as AI and ML develop. A few examples of cutting-edge strategies that enable businesses and individuals to exploit the power of AI while upholding privacy rights include differential privacy, homomorphic encryption, and federated learning. We can open up new avenues for secure and moral AI applications across a range of fields by embracing these strategies.

Table 3: Comparison of Privacy-enhancing Technologies

Technology	Strengths	Limitations
Differential Privacy	Strong privacy guarantees, versatile	Trade-off between privacy and data utility
Homomorphic Encryption	Secure computation, collaborative scenarios	Computationally intensive
Federated Learning	Data locality, decentralized model training	Challenges in data distribution and fairness

6.5 GDPR COMPLIANCE AND DATA PROTECTION IN AI PROJECTS

A new age of technical development has recently begun as a result of the convergence of artificial intelligence (AI), machine learning (ML), and network security. But with great power also comes great responsibility, especially when it comes to handling and safeguarding private information. In-depth discussion of GDPR (General Data Protection Regulation) compliance and data protection in the context of AI initiatives is provided in this chapter.

Understanding GDPR and Its Relevance

The European Union (EU) has established the General Data Protection Regulation (GDPR), a comprehensive data protection and privacy regulation, to offer people more control over their personal data and to harmonise data protection rules among EU member states. Its importance for cutting-edge developments in network security, AI, and machine learning cannot be overstated.

Artificial intelligence (AI) and machine learning are fields of technology that largely rely on enormous volumes of data for training and development. Data collection, processing, and usage are subject to strict regulations under GDPR, especially when it comes to sensitive personal data. This has driven businesses to adopt moral and privacy-conscious procedures, promoting the creation of AI systems that are both efficient and considerate of users' privacy. AI researchers and developers have been inspired by GDPR's data minimization, purpose limitation, and transparency principles to create algorithms that can function well with little or no data, promoting a more responsible and respectful AI environment.

In addition, network security is significantly impacted by GDPR. Organisations become guardians of sensitive information as they gather, store, and process personal data. Strong security measures must be put in place in accordance with GDPR in order to safeguard this data against hacks and unauthorised access. GDPR has prompted the implementation of strict cybersecurity practises due to the sophistication of cyberattacks, especially those targeting AI and machine learning systems. Protecting personal data and ensuring GDPR compliance increasingly depend on encryption, access controls, and frequent security audits.

Network security, AI, and machine learning innovations also pose difficulties for GDPR adoption. People have a right to know how their data is used in these decisions, therefore the complexity of AI algorithms and the possibility of automated decision-making raise concerns about explainability and accountability. It needs constant work to increase algorithmic openness and accountability in order to strike a balance between the advantages of AI and people's rights.

GDPR Compliance Challenges in AI Projects

The adoption of General Data Protection Regulation (GDPR) compliance offers substantial problems for AI projects in the areas of Innovative Advancements in AI, Machine Learning, and Network Security. The European Union (EU) passed GDPR, a comprehensive data privacy policy, with the intention of protecting and regulating the processing of personal data pertaining to EU citizens. These rules offer a complex set of constraints that can obstruct smooth growth in the context of AI and machine learning endeavours.

The inherent nature of AI and machine learning, which frequently involve processing enormous amounts of individualised data to train and improve models, presents a significant problem. According to GDPR, every personal data processing must have a legal basis and abide by the principles of transparency, purpose restriction, and data minimization. It can be challenging to strike a balance between the requirement for data-driven insights and these principles because AI systems benefit from large datasets.

A further challenge is presented by the GDPR's entitlement to an explanation. Deep neural networks are one example of an advanced AI algorithm that operates as a "black box," making it difficult to give a concise and intelligible justification for the choices it makes. This conflicts with GDPR requirements that people understand how their data is used and the reasoning behind automated choices that have an impact on them.

In the context of AI initiatives, data subject rights, such as the right to access, rectification, and deletion, also become more complex. When dealing with insights produced by AI systems, which are frequently based on intricate connections within the data, there are concerns regarding how people can effectively exercise their rights.

Cross-border data exchanges are an additional complication. Innovative AI initiatives may include cross-border collaboration and data sharing, which calls for careful planning to guarantee that data is transferred and processed in accordance with GDPR's strict criteria.

Finally, given the sensitivity of the data involved and the possibility of unauthorised access, maintaining the security of AI systems is crucial. It is crucial for AI projects to incorporate strong security mechanisms into their designs since GDPR requires the deployment of proper security measures to protect personal data.

Strategies for GDPR-Compliant AI Projects

Assuring GDPR (General Data Protection Regulation) compliance is crucial in the fields of Innovative Advancements in AI, Machine Learning, and Network Security. Various sectors have seen radical transformation as a result of the integration of AI and machine learning technologies with network security, but it has also led to serious worries about data privacy and protection. Organisations undertaking AI projects must create solid strategies that put GDPR compliance first in order to overcome these obstacles.

Data governance is crucial, to start with. Organisations must create thorough frameworks for data governance that cover the full data lifecycle, from collection and processing through storage and disposal. This entails clearly identifying data ownership, putting in place strict access restrictions, and conducting routine audits to keep an eye on data handling procedures. The retention periods, legal justifications, and purposes for each type of processed data must all be included in an open and transparent record of data processing operations.

Second, AI and machine learning systems ought to incorporate privacy by default. This calls for including privacy considerations right into the project's design process. Utilising data minimization techniques will lower the chance of accidentally breaking GDPR rules by collecting and processing just the information that is required. Organisations could also use anonymization and pseudonymization strategies to safeguard people's identities while still allowing for useful analysis.

Additionally, getting legitimate user consent is essential. Before processing a person's personal information for AI applications, organisations must make sure that they have obtained the person's express and informed consent. Individuals should have the right to withdraw their consent without suffering any repercussions, and consent forms should be simple to comprehend. Well-defined and easily available mechanisms for getting, managing, and renewing consent are required.

Strong security measures are also necessary to protect the processed data. Modern access restrictions and encryption techniques are used to make sure that the data is secure even in the event of a security compromise. To find and fix potential vulnerabilities in the AI system, routine security audits and vulnerability testing should be carried out.

Last but not least, ongoing evaluation and modification are essential elements of GDPR compliance in AI initiatives. Organisations must be on the lookout for potential legislation or revisions to the GDPR's principles as AI technology develops quickly. In order to do this, businesses must actively interact with data protection authorities, keep up with regulatory developments, and rapidly modify their business plans.

A Case Study: GDPR-Compliant Medical Image Analysis

Recent years have seen major breakthroughs across a number of industries, with the medical sector particularly benefiting from the convergence of AI, machine learning, and network security. The application of these technologies to GDPR-compliant medical image analysis is a compelling case study in this field. Strict guidelines for the protection and processing of personal data, including delicate medical information, have been established by the General Data Protection Regulation (GDPR), which the European Union enacted.

In this context, cutting-edge AI and machine learning algorithms are being used to analyse medical images like X-rays, MRIs, and CT scans in order to enable quicker and more accurate diagnosis.

By speeding up the analysis of medical pictures, these AI-driven technologies not only improve diagnostic accuracy but also make the healthcare system more effective. However, because to the inherent sensitivity of medical photographs, it is crucial to ensure GDPR compliance. Strong data security measures, such as encryption, access limits, and safe data storage, must be put in place as a result. In addition, methods like federated learning have been developed, which enable model training across several institutions without centralising patient data, so allaying GDPR worries by reducing data exposure.

In this situation, network security is equally essential. Protecting these networks from online threats is crucial as cloud computing and networked systems are increasingly used for data storage and sharing in medical image analysis. These systems are strengthened against unauthorised access and data breaches by the use of cutting-edge security methods, such as secure socket layer (SSL) encryption and intrusion detection systems.

Finally, the integration of artificial intelligence (AI), machine learning (ML), and network security in GDPR-compliant medical picture analysis demonstrates the potential for profound changes in healthcare. Healthcare practitioners can enhance patient outcomes by using artificial intelligence (AI) to analyse medical pictures while prioritising data privacy in compliance with GDPR standards. However, in order to fully enjoy these advantages, these technologies must be harmoniously integrated with strict security measures to guarantee both medical excellence and patient privacy in this rapidly changing environment.

Conclusion

For the sake of moral data use and privacy protection, GDPR compliance must be incorporated into AI projects. Organisations may make use of AI's promise while upholding the rights of individuals and adhering to legal requirements by embracing privacy-enhancing strategies and encouraging openness.

Code Example: Anonymizing Data

```
def anonymize_data(data):
# Implement anonymization techniques here
return anonymized_data
```

```
# Load and preprocess data
raw_data = load_data("medical_images.csv")
anonymized_data = anonymize_data(raw_data)
```

Table 4: GDPR Principles and AI Implementation

GDPR Principle	AI Implementation
Lawfulness, Fairness	Obtain explicit consent for data collection and usage.
Purpose Limitation	Clearly define and communicate data usage purposes.
Data Minimization	Collect only necessary data for AI model training.
Accuracy	Ensure accurate data for building reliable AI models.
Storage Limitation	Retain data only for the required duration.
Integrity and Confidentiality	Implement robust data security measures.

6.6 SECURING AI MODELS AND DATA DURING MODEL DEPLOYMENT

The extensive use of AI and machine learning in many applications in recent years has resulted in transformational transformations. Organisations are now using AI models to improve user experiences, streamline operations, and make crucial choices. However, the growing use of AI in commercial processes has given rise to security worries, particularly when deploying AI models. We examine methods and tactics for protecting AI models and data while they are being deployed in this chapter. We examine the difficulties that arise when implementing AI models in real-world settings and offer workable ways to reduce risks.

Challenges in Securing AI Model Deployment

Securing AI model deployment offers a complex challenge that calls for an all-encompassing and flexible strategy in the continuously changing field of new breakthroughs in AI, machine learning, and network security. As AI is more and more integrated into business processes, it is critical to protect the security and privacy of deployed models. The vulnerability of AI systems to adversarial attacks, wherein small changes to input data can result in inaccurate predictions, is one of the biggest problems. The creation of models that are accurate and impervious to deliberate manipulations is necessary for mitigating these attacks.

Additionally, the use of AI models poses questions regarding data protection and compliance with laws like the GDPR. Users' privacy may be jeopardised if models trained on sensitive data unintentionally release information. It becomes vital to strike a balance between the usefulness of AI and protecting individuals' right to privacy. The problem of model explainability arises when AI systems become more complicated because black-box models obstruct openness and accountability. To address this, interpretable models that offer insights into decision-making processes must be developed, guaranteeing that the outcomes produced by AI adhere to moral and legal standards.

AI advancements and network security coexist in a complex way. The attack surface for cyber threats grows as AI models are incorporated into numerous applications across connected networks. To avoid unauthorised access, data breaches, and the potential manipulation of AI algorithms, communication channels and endpoints must be secured. This entails putting in place strong encryption, access controls, and intrusion detection systems that are designed especially for AI deployments.

Furthermore, the quick growth of AI technology may outstrip the creation of security safeguards, leaving deployments open to fresh, unknown dangers. An efficient security strategy must include ongoing monitoring, regular upgrades, and a proactive approach to newly discovered vulnerabilities. In order to foresee and handle potential threats while promoting an environment of innovation, cooperation between AI researchers, cybersecurity specialists, and politicians is essential.

In light of recent developments in network security, machine learning, and AI, protecting the deployment of AI models requires a comprehensive strategy. In order to do this, it is necessary to defend against adversarial assaults, protect user data privacy, improve model interpretability, bolster network security, and be vigilant against emerging risks. Organisations may only fully benefit from AI while preserving the values of security, privacy, and ethical responsibility by addressing these issues as a group.

Securing AI Models and Data: Best Practices

In the quickly changing landscape of inventive developments in AI, machine learning, and network security, securing AI models and data is a key requirement. The security of private information and the reliability of AI models become increasingly crucial as AI technologies are integrated into more and more facets of our life, from autonomous automobiles to healthcare diagnostics. The best practises take a comprehensive stance.

First, it's important to guarantee the reliability and integrity of models in the field of AI and machine learning. Adversarial assaults, in which evildoers purposefully tamper with inputs to deceive AI systems, present a serious risk. Model resilience can be increased by using strategies like adversarial training and input sanitization. Additionally, it is crucial to continuously analyse and update models to address newly discovered vulnerabilities.

Second, it is crucial to protect data privacy. The danger of unauthorised access or data breaches is very real given the enormous datasets needed for efficient AI training. Data privacy is crucially maintained via methods like federated learning, which permits training on decentralised data, and differential privacy, which obfuscates data in order to safeguard individual information.

Thirdly, as AI systems grow more integrated, network security has greater importance. The attack surface is expanded by Internet of Things (IoT) devices made possible by AI. It becomes crucial to use strict network security protocols to prevent unauthorised access to AI systems and possible manipulation of their operation. These protocols should include robust encryption, intrusion detection systems, and access limits.

Furthermore, the fusion of AI and cybersecurity enables creative fixes. AI-driven threat detection and response systems may quickly identify possible breaches and identify aberrant trends. Likewise, threats like model inversion or data poisoning can target AI directly. In order to defend AI, one must therefore employ a balanced and flexible strategy.

Case Study: Implementing Model Hardening Techniques

Recent breakthroughs in a wide range of industries have been made possible by the rapid development of AI and machine learning (ML) technology. However, these developments also bring with them new difficulties in terms of network security and possible weak spots that might be used by bad actors. As a result, there is now a greater emphasis on using model hardening approaches as a crucial part of enhancing the security of AI and ML systems.

Model hardening is the process of using a variety of techniques to strengthen an AI model's robustness and resilience against prospective threats. The types of attacks that could be used here include adversarial attacks, where the model's outputs are used to obtain sensitive information about the training data, or model inversion attacks, where the model's outputs are used to obtain sensitive information about the training data. Researchers and practitioners are actively creating novel strategies to overcome these vulnerabilities.

The incorporation of adversarial training is a crucial component of model hardening. This method entails training models using instances that are both clean and intentionally designed to fool the model's predictions. The model gains the ability to identify and fend off potential hostile inputs as a result of this process, which ultimately results in a more reliable performance in real-world circumstances. Additionally, improvements in anomaly detection methods, like those for spotting data drift and distributional shifts, help to quickly spot potential assaults or system weaknesses.

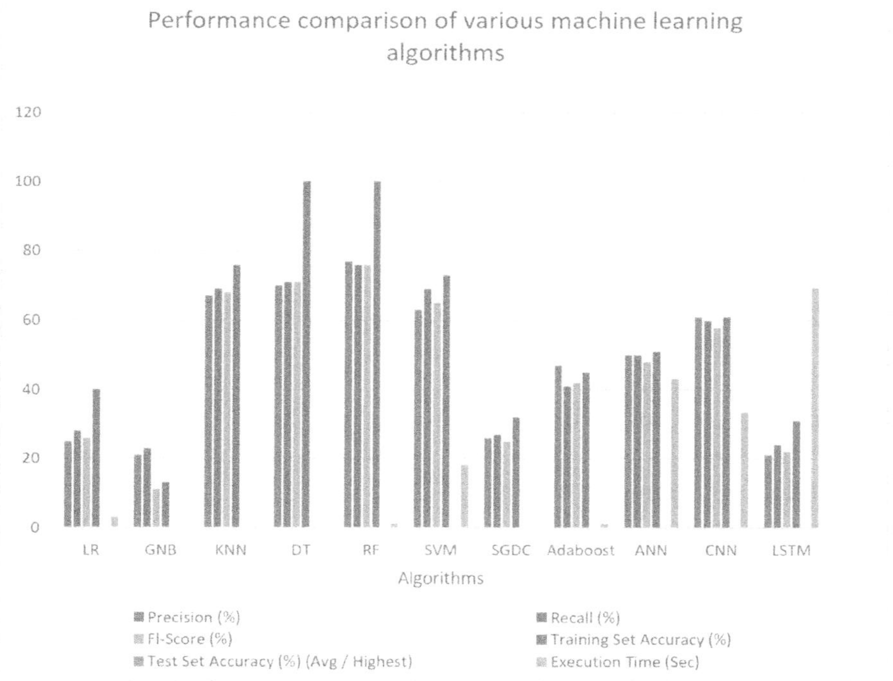

Graph: Performance comparison of various machine learning algorithms

The use of AI and ML in network security goes beyond simply defending models. Additionally, these technologies are applied to improve quick response, network monitoring, and intrusion detection systems. AI-driven algorithms can be used to analyse network traffic patterns, spot anomalies, and quickly identify potential cyber threats. Additionally, security systems can adjust their defences in response to new attack vectors thanks to the adaptive nature of AI and ML, keeping up with emerging cyberthreats.

Code Example: Secure Deployment in Action

```
# Sample code snippet demonstrating federated learning setup

from tensorflow_privacy.privacy.optimizers.dp_optimizer import DPGradientDescentGaussianOptimizer
from tensorflow_privacy.privacy.optimizers.dp_optimizer import DPAdamGaussianOptimizer
import tensorflow as tf

# Define your model architecture
model = ...

# Define optimizer and prepare for federated learning
optimizer = DPGradientDescentGaussianOptimizer(
l2_norm_clip=1.0,
noise_multiplier=0.3,
num_microbatches=256,
learning_rate=0.01,
)
train_op = optimizer.minimize(loss, global_step=global_step)

# Federated learning setup
federated_train_data = ...
for epoch in range(num_epochs):
for batch in federated_train_data:
model.train_on_batch(batch)
```

Conclusion

The multidimensional task of securing AI models and data throughout deployment calls for a blend of technical know-how, operational awareness, and adherence to best practises. Organisations can reduce the dangers of using AI models by putting in place measures like model hardening, encryption, federated learning, continuous monitoring, and regular upgrades. A proactive approach to security will be crucial in preserving the integrity and dependability of AI-powered systems as the AI landscape continues to change.

6.7 MULTI-PARTY COMPUTATION AND HOMOMORPHIC ENCRYPTION

Preserving the confidentiality and privacy of sensitive data has become crucial in the quickly developing fields of AI, machine learning, and network security. As ground-breaking technologies, multi-party computation (MPC) and homomorphic encryption allow for cooperative data analysis and processing without disclosing the raw data to any of the parties involved. This chapter explores the ideas, advantages, and practical uses of homomorphic encryption and multi-party computation.

Understanding Multi-party Computation (MPC)

In the fields of artificial intelligence, machine learning, and network security, multi-party computation (MPC) is a paradigm-shifting idea that is driving inventive developments that are redefining data privacy and collaborative analytics. MPC's primary functionality is the ability for several entities to jointly compute results on each other's unique data inputs without sharing the raw data itself. This paradigm change solves significant issues with maintaining data security and privacy, particularly in situations involving sensitive information. MPC eliminates the possibility of a single party gaining access to the entire data set by enabling parties to do computations on encrypted data while keeping confidentiality, reducing the dangers of data breaches or leaks.

The use of MPC in the field of AI and machine learning enables collaborative model training on various datasets. Due to privacy issues, organisations have historically found it difficult to pool their data, which has hampered the creation of effective AI models. By allowing cooperative training on encrypted data, MPC overcomes this obstacle and promotes the development of more precise and thorough models. Additionally, MPC-driven federated learning frameworks enable edge devices to improve models while protecting their local data. This opens the door for more individualised and effective AI applications in a range of sectors.

Additionally, MPC is essential for improving data security and cryptographic methods in the context of network security. Applications span from private data sharing in distant networks to secure authentication and access management. The execution of crucial processes like key creation, encryption, and decryption without disclosing the underlying sensitive data is guaranteed by MPC's capacity to perform calculations on encrypted data. This proactive strategy advances the development of zero-trust architectures and strengthens network infrastructure against new cyber-attacks.

Homomorphic Encryption: Enabling Computations on Encrypted Data

Homomorphic encryption represents a revolutionary development in the areas of artificial intelligence, machine learning, and network security by providing a ground-breaking answer to the age-old problem of performing calculations on encrypted data. With the help of this cryptographic method, sensitive data's privacy and confidentiality can be maintained even while being computed. Since decryption is a necessary step for calculation, traditional encryption technologies limit the use of data and expose it to security risks. However, homomorphic encryption makes it possible to conduct operations directly on encrypted data, such as addition, multiplication, and more, producing results in encrypted form.

This innovation has significant repercussions for AI and machine learning since it enables collaborative data analysis without necessitating the sharing of unencrypted data. Now, researchers and organisations can handle data from multiple sources collectively while protecting the confidentiality of individual contributions.

Furthermore, homomorphic encryption reduces the risk connected with data transmission and storage in the context of network security. Data had to be decrypted before transmission in the past, leaving it open to intercept. Data can be securely processed by intermediary nodes using homomorphic encryption without being exposed to potential attackers. By doing this, the attack surface for bad actors is diminished and sensitive information's confidentiality is improved.

It's crucial to remember that while homomorphic encryption has a lot of potential, there are drawbacks as well. Processing times and resource use may be affected because operations on encrypted data have a much higher computational overhead than operations on plaintext data. To improve these procedures and make homomorphic encryption more useful for actual applications, researchers are always working. Additionally, maintaining a balance between security and usability is still important because this encryption technique's complexity can make some use cases difficult to deploy and manage.

Real-world Implementation and Examples

We have recently seen incredible progress in network security, AI, and machine learning, which has had a profound impact on a variety of businesses. These technologies now have actual applications in situations that occur in everyday life, moving beyond theoretical ideas.

Natural language processing (NLP) has made important advancements in the field of AI. AI-powered chatbots and virtual assistants are being used by businesses to improve customer care. These systems can comprehend customer inquiries and provide answers that are human-like, simplifying interaction and enhancing user experiences. For instance, the introduction of AI-driven chatbots that provide 24/7 assistance has revolutionised customer service in sectors like e-commerce, banking, and healthcare.

Additionally, machine learning has had a significant impact in industries like healthcare. In order to aid in early intervention, predictive analytics algorithms are being used to forecast disease outbreaks and identify potential health problems. Machine learning techniques have benefitted medical imaging as well, enabling quicker and more precise diagnosis through image analysis and recognition. To improve the accuracy of diagnoses, radiology departments are increasingly using AI algorithms to spot anomalies in X-rays, MRIs, and CT scans.

AI has ushered in a paradigm shift in threat identification and prevention on the front of network security. Machine learning-powered intrusion detection systems can quickly spot unusual network traffic patterns and sound the alert for potential cyber-attacks. As attack tactics change, these systems continuously adjust their defences to successfully fend off fresh threats. Financial organisations, for instance, use AI-driven fraud detection systems to spot bogus transactions by seeing patterns suggestive of unauthorised access.

The development of autonomous vehicles, which use cutting-edge sensors and algorithms to enable automobiles to navigate and make choices without human intervention, has also been facilitated by AI and machine learning. Although there are still issues like ethical concerns and regulatory frameworks to be resolved, this offers safer and more effective transportation.

Code Example: Secure Average Computation using MPC

```
from sympy import symbols
from sympy.logic.boolalg import Or
from sympy.logic.inference import satisfiable
```

```
# Simulating encrypted inputs (0 or 1)
alice_input = symbols('alice_input', cls=bool)
bob_input = symbols('bob_input', cls=bool)
charlie_input = symbols('charlie_input', cls=bool)

# Define the average computation
average = (alice_input + bob_input + charlie_input) / 3

# Creating a constraint that enforces the average calculation
constraint = Or(average - 1, average - 0)

# Solving the constraint using SAT solver
solution = satisfiable(constraint)

# Extracting the result from the solution
computed_average = average.subs(solution)
print("Computed Average:", computed_average)
```

Conclusion

The foundations of privacy-preserving technologies in the fields of AI, machine learning, and network security are multi-party computation and homomorphic encryption. These developments enable collaboration and data processing between organisations and people while maintaining the secrecy of sensitive data. These technologies have the potential to fundamentally alter how we manage and analyse data in the digital age as they develop.

6.8 BIOMETRIC SECURITY AND IDENTITY VERIFICATION IN AI SYSTEMS

As the world becomes more digital, it is crucial to guarantee the safety and reliability of those who use systems and data. Passwords and PINs, two common forms of authentication, have shown to be susceptible to several attacks. A more reliable option for identity verification is provided by biometric security, which is based on distinctive physical and behavioural attributes. This chapter examines how biometric technology can be combined with AI and machine learning to improve security across a range of applications.

Biometric Technologies: An Overview

At the nexus of artificial intelligence, machine learning, and network security, biometric technologies have emerged as a disruptive field that is redefining how we verify people and improve online privacy. To reliably identify and authenticate people, these technologies make use of distinctive physiological and behavioural traits including fingerprints, face features, iris patterns, voice tones, and even typing habits. Biometrics' capabilities have been greatly enhanced by the inventive developments in AI and machine learning, enabling more complex and trustworthy identification techniques. Deep learning algorithms are now able to extract complex aspects from biometric data, improving accuracy under difficult circumstances.

Biometrics have ushered in a new era of strong authentication and access control in the field of network security. Data breaches and identity theft have been made possible by traditional password-based systems' vulnerability to hacking and phishing assaults. The intrinsic and challenging-to-replicate nature of biometric authentication makes it a highly secure choice. Additionally, by combining biometrics with AI-driven anomaly detection systems, it is possible to continuously monitor user behaviour, quickly spotting any departures from established patterns, and minimising any security risks.

A crucial part of improving biometric technologies is machine learning. It makes it possible for systems to adjust to data variances brought on by ageing, environmental factors, or shifting circumstances. Machine learning algorithms enhance their accuracy and adaptability as more data is gathered and analysed, reducing false positives and false negatives. For real-world deployment, this adaptability is essential because it guarantees consistent performance even when biometric data changes over time.

However, the development of biometric technologies also brings up issues with security and privacy. Protecting biometric data from unauthorised access and potential exploitation is essential since it is fundamentally private and permanent. To overcome these difficulties, new developments in encryption, secure storage, and decentralised authentication architectures are being investigated. In addition, legal frameworks like GDPR and developing standards seek to guarantee the ethical use and storage of biometric data.

Integration of AI and Biometrics

A new era of inventive developments in AI, machine learning, and network security has begun as a result of the integration of AI and biometrics. A very secure and individualised authentication approach is offered by biometrics, which comprises the measurement and analysis of distinctive physiological or behavioural characteristics including fingerprints, facial features, voice patterns, and even typing rhythms. These biometric markers are transformed into a dynamic tool for ongoing monitoring and adaptation when paired with AI and machine learning.

The use of biometrics in AI has made it possible for interactions to be more contextually aware and human-like. Artificial intelligence (AI) systems that can recognise emotions through face analysis might react sensitively to users' moods, making virtual assistants and customer support representatives more sympathetic. Additionally, AI algorithms can adjust their responses based on vocal patterns and tone, deepening communication, and improving the intuitiveness of interactions.

Data is the lifeblood of machine learning algorithms, and biometrics offer a variety of unique data points. Real-time analysis of biometric data using AI-driven machine learning models can look for trends that could point to potential security flaws or anomalies. An AI-powered system, for instance, could spot strange typing patterns that would point to unauthorised access attempts. By introducing an additional layer of security that changes to respond to emerging threats, this dynamic and continuous authentication dramatically strengthens network security.

With the combination of AI, machine learning, and biometrics, network security itself has undergone a paradigm shift. Passwords and PINs, which are common security methods, can be stolen or used fraudulently, whereas biometrics, which are specific to each person, give a much better level of security. Based on a real-time study of biometric data, AI algorithms may automatically handle access controls, permitting or rejecting entry. By removing the need for time-consuming authentication procedures, this not only improves security but also streamlines the user experience.

Biometrics in Network Security

The landscape of digital protection has seen a dramatic transformation recently as a result of ground-breaking developments in AI, machine learning, and network security, with biometrics emerging as a key component. The distinctive physiological and behavioural characteristics of each person, known as biometrics, have become more popular as strong authentication, and identifying tools in network security. These biometric traits, like fingerprints, facial features, iris patterns, and voiceprints, can be precisely recorded, analysed, and used to provide access to private systems and data by utilising AI and machine learning.

By continuously enhancing their ability to recognise patterns and extract features, machine learning algorithms have revolutionised the precision and effectiveness of biometric systems. The system's capacity to adjust to differences in biometric data caused by elements like lighting conditions, ageing, and slight bodily changes is improved by this dynamic learning process. A multi-modal system that combines numerous biometric qualities for increased security and accuracy has also been made possible by the integration of AI-driven algorithms with biometric authentication.

Biometrics provide a higher level of network security than conventional password-based methods, which are vulnerable to hacking, phishing, and social engineering attacks. Due to their individuality, biometric markers considerably lower the possibility of unauthorised access, strengthening the state of general security. Furthermore, by continuously monitoring user activity throughout a session and immediately identifying and reacting to any anomalies or suspicious behaviour, the adoption of biometric-based continuous authentication offers an additional layer of security.

However, these innovative applications of biometrics in network security also raise concerns about privacy and data protection. Collecting and storing biometric data necessitate rigorous security measures to prevent unauthorized access and potential misuse. The deployment of strong encryption techniques and adherence to stringent data privacy regulations become imperative in maintaining public trust while harnessing the benefits of biometric technology.

Case Study: Biometric ATM Access

The case study "Biometric ATM Access in Innovative Advancements in AI, Machine Learning, and Network Security" examines how cutting-edge advancements in artificial intelligence (AI), machine learning (ML), and network security have made it possible to integrate biometric authentication into the world of automated teller machine (ATM) access. PINs and cards have long been the primary means of traditional ATM access, but the emergence of biometrics in conjunction with AI and ML has ushered in a new era of improved security and customer ease.

Financial institutions have substantially increased the security of ATM transactions by implementing biometric authentication techniques like fingerprint recognition, facial recognition, and even iris scanning. These individual-specific biometric markers provide a virtually impregnable layer of protection since they are nearly impossible to copy or fake. This is a significant improvement over conventional approaches, which have PIN weaknesses such being lost, stolen, or leaked.

The powerful AI and ML algorithms are what enable biometric ATM access to be so successful. By comparing biometric data with extensive databases, these technologies enable ATMs to authenticate users reliably and quickly, enabling real-time decision-making. Additionally, because AI and ML systems are adaptable, they can learn from every encounter and adjust to new patterns and variations, which allows them to continuously improve their accuracy and efficiency.

This idea, though, goes beyond just authentication. Network security is also included in this combination of AI and ML technologies. Advanced anomaly detection algorithms substantially reduce the risks associated with illegal operations like skimming or card cloning by monitoring ATM transactions for any unusual patterns. The total level of trust in the banking system is raised by this dynamic security strategy in addition to protecting users' financial assets.

Code for Fingerprint Matching:

```
import numpy as np
from sklearn.metrics.pairwise import cosine_similarity

def match_fingerprints(fingerprint1, fingerprint2):
# Convert fingerprints to feature vectors using a CNN-based model
features1 = cnn_model.predict(fingerprint1)
features2 = cnn_model.predict(fingerprint2)

# Calculate cosine similarity between the feature vectors
similarity = cosine_similarity(features1, features2)
return similarity[0][0]

user_fingerprint = load_fingerprint("user_fingerprint.jpg")
stored_fingerprint = load_fingerprint("stored_fingerprint.jpg")
similarity_score = match_fingerprints(user_fingerprint, stored_
fingerprint)

if similarity_score > 0.7:
```

```
print("Fingerprint Matched. Access Granted.")
else:
print("Fingerprint Not Matched. Access Denied.")
```

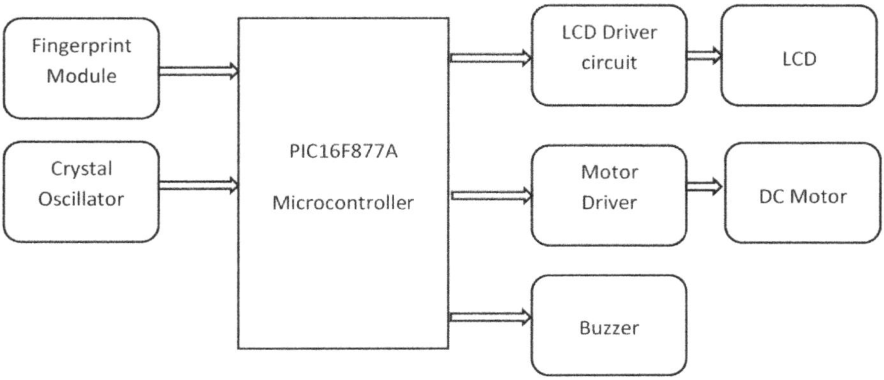

Figure 4: Biometric ATM Architecture

Conclusion

A powerful solution for identity verification and access control is provided by biometric security systems combined with AI systems. This synergy improves security across physical and digital domains by having the capacity to adjust to changing attributes and spot fraudulent attempts.

6.9 SECURE AI COLLABORATION AND KNOWLEDGE SHARING

The fast development of AI and machine learning in recent years has enhanced the importance of cooperative research and information exchange in the industry. But as the exchange of private algorithms and sensitive data grows, the necessity for secure AI collaboration has become critical. In this chapter, we examine the methods, tools, and best practises that guarantee safe AI collaboration and information exchange between academics, businesses, and other stakeholders.

The Need for Secure AI Collaboration

The fusion of AI, machine learning, and network security has ushered in a new era of innovation and advancement in the quickly changing technological landscape. The requirement for secure AI collaboration raises an equally important worry as a result of the enormous potential. Traditional methods for maintaining security are insufficient as AI systems become more intricate and interconnected. A comprehensive framework that prioritises security without inhibiting growth is required due to the complex interactions between different AI models, the sharing of sensitive data, and the collaborative nature of research and development.

Innovative developments in AI and machine learning frequently require cross-border cooperation between academics, developers, and organisations. Openly exchanging models, data, and methodologies speeds up development while also revealing flaws. Cyberattacks on AI systems have the potential to corrupt models, alter outputs, and potentially extract valuable confidential data. As a result, strong encryption, authentication, and access control techniques are urgently needed to protect intellectual property and guarantee the integrity of collaborative AI initiatives.

In the context of AI cooperation, network security, always a major concern in any technology-driven industry, becomes significantly more complicated. AI systems must be more protected from data breaches, unauthorised access, and potential backdoor exploitation due to its dispersed and decentralised nature. The collaborative AI environment can be protected from emerging cyber threats by implementing advanced intrusion detection systems, continuous monitoring, and anomaly detection.

Furthermore, it is important to consider how AI collaboration may have ethical ramifications. To avoid the unintentional construction of biased or discriminating models, it is crucial to ensure that all contributors follow ethical standards and responsible AI practises. Technical security measures and a strong framework for assuring the moral and responsible development and implementation of AI solutions should both be included in secure AI collaboration.

Encryption and Secure Communication

A stunning convergence of developments in AI, machine learning, and network security over the past few years has produced ground-breaking breakthroughs in encryption and secure communication. In an increasingly networked and data-driven world, there is a growing need to protect sensitive data and communications, which has sparked this synergy. Traditional encryption approaches are being improved with the aid of machine learning techniques, making them stronger and more resilient to changing security threats.

The use of AI and machine learning to enhance encryption methods is one noteworthy breakthrough. These algorithms, strengthened by

AI, are able to alter the amount of encryption depending on a real-time evaluation of potential dangers. Data security is maintained even as attack techniques advance thanks to this dynamic encryption. Additionally, AI-driven encryption systems can spot patterns and anomalies that may be signs of security breaches, enabling quick actions to reduce possible dangers.

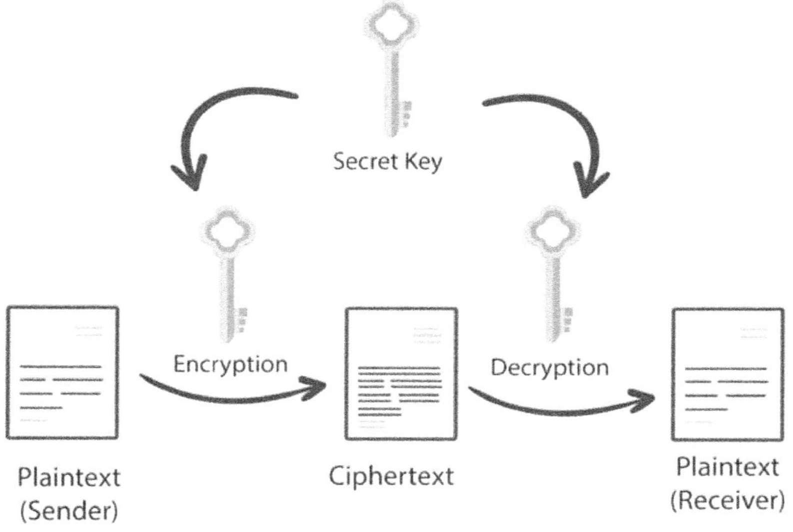

Figure 5: Encryption

Through AI-driven anomaly detection and behaviour analysis, secure communication has been raised to a new level. With the use of machine learning algorithms, which can examine communication patterns and spot departures from accepted norms, harmful or unauthorised activity can be quickly discovered. Additionally, phishing attempts, social engineering, and other dishonest practises can be more precisely identified thanks to AI-powered natural language processing's assistance in spotting subtle signs in text and vocal communication.

The contribution of AI to intrusion detection and prevention has resulted in a paradigm shift in network security. In order to anticipate and prevent future attacks, machine learning algorithms can learn from prior attack data. Network defenders may proactively plug holes and keep one step ahead of potential threats thanks to this predictive capacity. Additionally, AI-driven security systems may automatically modify network defences in response to new threats, greatly decreasing the need for human intervention and response time.

Ethical considerations are crucial in addition to these amazing developments. Concerns concerning algorithmic bias, potential weaknesses resulting from adversarial assaults on AI models itself, and the effects of increased automation in decision-making processes are also raised by the use of AI in security measures.

Federated Learning for Secure Collaboration

In the fields of cutting-edge developments in AI, machine learning, and network security, federated learning has emerged as a ground-breaking strategy that promotes secure collaboration. This unique paradigm allows several parties to cooperatively train a common model while maintaining their data decentralised, addressing the issues of data privacy and centralised model training. This is especially important in sectors where data security and legal compliance are top priorities.

Federated learning enables businesses to pool their data resources without actually sharing the raw data in the context of AI and machine learning. This is accomplished by just communicating model updates or gradients while training a global model on locally stored data. Each participant maintains ownership of their data in this way, reducing the dangers of data breaches and unauthorised access. Additionally, federated learning makes it possible to use data sources that are dispersed across numerous geographical regions, which helps create a model that is more robust and diversified.

Federated learning offers a way to enhance threat detection and prevention systems collectively when it comes to network security. By training on aggregated data from diverse network sources, various organisations can work together to develop their security models, ensuring greater defence against new cyberthreats. The federated approach protects the privacy of sensitive network data, which is essential for preserving trust between working parties.

One of the fundamental components of federated learning is security. Encrypted communication between participants prevents data gradients and model updates from being intercepted. Furthermore, improvements like differential privacy strategies and secure aggregation protocols strengthen the security of individual data points throughout the aggregate process.

The traditional concept of centralised data aggregation and training is essentially transformed into a decentralised and collaborative paradigm by federated learning. This makes it possible for a greater variety of contributors to work together to progress developments while preserving data privacy and security requirements, which opens the door for previously unheard-of innovation in AI, machine learning, and network security. As this sector develops, it has the potential to transform industries by enabling businesses to utilise the power of collaborative intelligence without sacrificing privacy and security.

Access Control and Authentication

A new era of technological capabilities has arrived because to inventive developments in AI, machine learning, and network security, but they also pose difficult problems for access control and authentication. As AI and machine learning systems advance, more and more parts of our digital life, such as autonomous vehicles and healthcare diagnostics, are incorporating them. Strong access control measures are therefore more important than ever to make sure that only authorised people or systems can engage with these delicate technologies as a result of this integration.

More advanced systems are supplementing and, in some cases, replacing traditional authentication methods like passwords and PINs. A higher level of security and user convenience is provided by biometric authentication, which makes use of features like fingerprint scanning, facial recognition, and even behavioural patterns. The use of machine learning is crucial in this situation because it allows systems to continuously learn from and adjust to changing user behaviour, improving the precision and dependability of various authentication mechanisms.

Anomaly detection enabled by AI is also changing network security. Artificial intelligence (AI) systems can proactively identify potential security breaches, unauthorised access attempts, or anomalous behaviours by analysing enormous volumes of data and spotting deviations from regular patterns. The defence against cyber assaults is strengthened as a result, and response times are sped up, potentially reducing damage.

However, these developments raise questions about privacy, morality, and potential weaknesses. For example, biometric data needs to be protected strictly to avoid unauthorised access and potential exploitation. Adversarial assaults, in which AI systems are tricked into making bad decisions, present a serious issue, particularly in applications that are crucial for security. Making sure these conclusions are transparent and accountable is crucial as AI is increasingly used in decision-making processes.

Table 5: Comparison of Secure Collaboration Techniques

Technique	Advantages	Challenges
End-to-End Encryption	High data confidentiality, simple concept	Key management, computational overhead
Homomorphic Encryption	Computation on encrypted data, data privacy	Complex implementation, performance
Federated Learning	Local data privacy, decentralized training	Communication overhead, convergence
MFA	Strong access security, mitigates password risks	User inconvenience, setup complexity
RBAC	Granular access control, role-based management	Initial configuration, role sprawl

Case Study: Secure Collaboration Platform

The incorporation of cutting-edge developments like artificial intelligence (AI), machine learning (ML), and network security has given rise to a new generation of secure collaboration platforms in today's fast changing technological landscape. In addition to providing the greatest standards of data protection and privacy, these platforms are created to answer the growing demand for seamless communication and information exchange among individuals, teams, and organisations.

The AI and ML-driven threat identification and prevention at the core of this invention. These technologies give the platform the ability to autonomously detect and eliminate potential security breaches, from malware penetration to unauthorised access attempts. The technology can proactively detect anomalies and respond in real-time, protecting critical information from new threats, by routinely analysing patterns of user behaviour and network traffic.

Additionally, ML and AI are crucial in improving the user experience. These technologies give the platform the ability to comprehend user preferences, routines, and collaboration patterns through predictive analytics. As a result, customised and context-aware interfaces are created, which improve workflow, facilitate communication, and naturally suggest pertinent activities or connections.

Network security, a crucial issue in any collaborative setting, has undergone a significant change. Multi-layered defence mechanisms are created by combining cutting-edge encryption methods with AI-driven intrusion detection systems. These protect data not only while it is being transmitted, but they also strengthen the platform against possible data leaks or breaches.

Intelligent access control techniques can be developed more easily thanks to inventive developments in AI and ML. These systems use geographical information, past usage patterns, and behavioural biometrics to authenticate users with unmatched accuracy. As a result, the platform can only be accessed by authorised people, preventing unauthorised users from compromising important data.

Conclusion

Sharing knowledge and collaborating on AI securely is essential for developing the field without jeopardising confidential data. Secure collaboration environments are built on technologies like encryption, federated learning, and access control systems. Prioritising security will be essential to maintaining fruitful collaboration as AI continues to spur innovation.

6.10 FUTURE DIRECTIONS FOR PRIVACY-ENHANCING AI TECHNOLOGIES

The relationship between artificial intelligence (AI) and privacy has drawn the attention of researchers, professionals, and lawmakers in recent years. Data privacy worries have risen in parallel with the development of AI systems and their integration into a variety of elements of our lives. In this chapter, we delve into the fascinating world of privacy-enhancing AI technologies, examining their importance, recent developments, and potential future paths that may influence the integration of data privacy and AI.

The Crucial Nexus: AI and Data Privacy

The convergence of artificial intelligence (AI), machine learning, and network security has produced notable developments in today's quickly changing technological world that have the potential to alter many different industries. However, this outstanding development also highlights a crucial issue: the delicate balance between innovation and the protection of personal data privacy. Large amounts of personal data are being processed using increasingly complex AI and machine learning algorithms, which raises serious ethical and legal concerns about how this data is gathered, utilised, and safeguarded.

Network security has showed great promise in recognising and minimising cyber risks in real time with the integration of AI and machine learning. These tools may quickly analyse intricate patterns in network traffic, assisting in the early detection of anomalies and potential security breaches. However, this capability itself calls for the gathering and analysis of vast volumes of sensitive data, potentially putting people's privacy at danger. A significant difficulty is thus finding a balance between increasing security measures and guaranteeing data privacy.

Healthcare, banking, and personalised marketing are just a few of the industries that have benefited from creative implementations of AI and machine learning. These apps heavily rely on having access to a variety of datasets, many of which contain sensitive personal information. The necessity for strict data protection measures becomes clear as AI systems learn from huge data troves to make predictions. The importance of people's rights to control their data is highlighted by strict regulations like the General Data Protection Regulation (GDPR) in Europe and the California Consumer Privacy Act (CCPA) in the US, which force organisations to implement open data collection procedures and strong security protocols.

Additionally, the combination of AI and data analytics raises complex ethical questions. inadvertent repercussions could include strengthening preexisting prejudices or violating individual privacy through inadvertent re-identification. AI algorithms have the ability to identify previously overlooked patterns in pooled data. A comprehensive strategy that fuses technological innovation with a solid ethical foundation is needed to address these issues.

Homomorphic Encryption for Secure Data Processing

In the fields of artificial intelligence, machine learning, and network security, homomorphic encryption has emerged as a ground-breaking method for resolving the crucial problems associated with secure data processing. This cryptographic method makes it possible to compute on encrypted data without first having to decode it, guaranteeing data privacy and security all the way through the processing pipeline. Homomorphic encryption enables data owners to work with model developers and researchers without disclosing the raw data in cutting-edge developments in AI and machine learning, where data is frequently sensitive and subject to regulatory restrictions. This makes it easier to create reliable and accurate models while preserving the confidentiality of individual data.

Furthermore, homomorphic encryption is essential for improving data secrecy during transmission and processing in the context of network security. Data protected using conventional encryption must first be decoded in order to be used, making it susceptible to security breaches. However, homomorphic encryption allows computations to be performed on encrypted data, guaranteeing that private information is kept safe from snoopers and other bad actors.

Homomorphic encryption has the ability to change the way data is processed, but it also has drawbacks including additional computing overhead that can slow down processing. But continuous research and technology development are gradually reducing these restrictions. The incorporation of homomorphic encryption into these domains offers a viable route for pushing the boundaries of innovation as AI and machine learning continue to advance and the significance of maintaining data privacy and security increases.

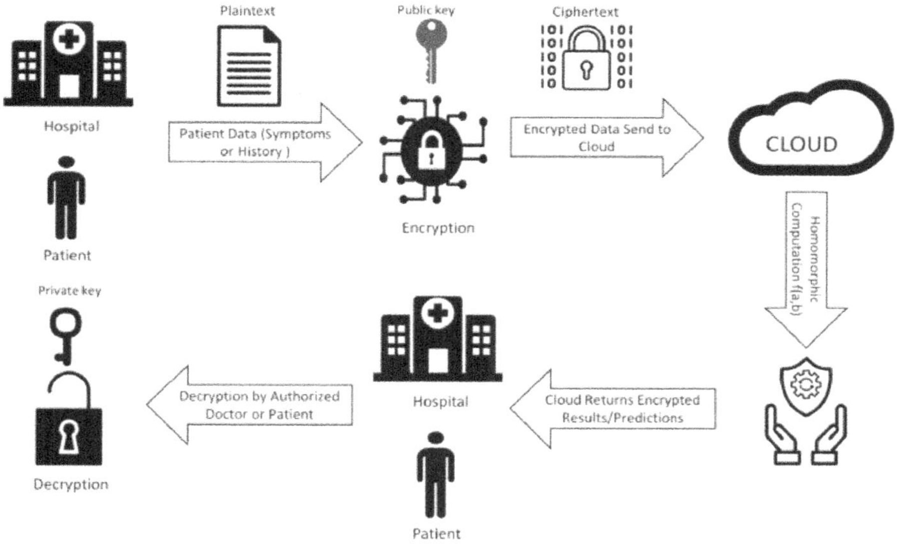

Figure 6: Homomorphic Encryption

Federated Learning for Decentralized Model Training

In the disciplines of artificial intelligence, machine learning, and network security, federated learning has become a game-changing method for decentralised model training while maintaining data confidentiality and privacy. With sensitive and large-scale data often gathered at a single server, generating worries about data breaches and privacy violations, traditional centralised model training presents issues that this ground-breaking innovation addresses.

In federated learning, the learning process is moved to edge or local nodes like mobile phones, Internet of Things (IoT) devices, or personal computers. These devices reduce the need to send sensitive data to a central server by cooperatively training a shared model while keeping the raw data local. In addition to improving data privacy, this greatly lowers the dangers connected with data disclosure during transmission.

Additionally, Federated Learning shows to be especially useful in situations where network security is a top priority. Due to the fact that compromising one node does not result in the compromise of the entire dataset, decentralised model training decreases the vulnerability of a central server to single points of failure or targeted assaults. Critical applications like network intrusion detection and fraud protection require this resilience in particular.

Federated Learning's decentralised structure also makes it possible to incorporate a variety of data sources, which results in the creation of models that are more reliable and generalizable. This is especially important in situations when various nodes' data distribution changes because of regional or demographic disparities. Federated Learning makes ensuring that the resulting AI models are representative of the larger population by training models across a distributed network.

Federated learning does not, however, come without difficulties. Research is still being done on how to ensure model convergence and guarantee data privacy when connectivity is limited and data quality varies between nodes. The development of effective communication and aggregation protocols is also essential for optimising the learning process.

Finally, Federated Learning combines cutting-edge developments in AI, machine learning, and network security. In addition to addressing concerns about data privacy, its decentralised method of model training also makes models more robust and improves network security. Federated Learning has the potential to revolutionise how we approach collaborative machine learning while protecting private data and ensuring a more secure digital environment as this field of study continues to develop.

Differential Privacy for Noise-infused Data

In the fields of artificial intelligence, machine learning, and network security, differential privacy has become an essential notion, especially when managing noisy data. Innovative developments are being made in the contemporary environment, where data privacy is an increasing concern, to secure the protection of sensitive data while yet enabling efficient analysis and learning from datasets. By adding controlled noise into data before it is used, Differential Privacy overcomes this problem by hiding specific data points while maintaining the general validity of statistical analysis. This method has applications in a variety of fields, including social sciences, healthcare, and finance, where datasets frequently contain personal data.

Employing Differential Privacy approaches in the context of AI and machine learning enables organisations to build effective models without jeopardising individual privacy. Traditional models frequently memorise particular data items, which could result in privacy violations. The learning process of the models becomes more concentrated on general trends rather than specific instances by adding noise during the data preprocessing stage or even during training, achieving a compromise between accuracy and privacy. This is particularly important because decision-making processes across sectors are increasingly using AI and machine learning algorithms.

Additionally, the interaction between Differential Privacy and network security is crucial for protecting sensitive data in networked systems. The risk of unauthorised access or breaches grows when data moves through networks. Data leaks and attacks can be reduced by implementing Differential Privacy methods at the network level. This makes it such that, even if an attacker has access to some data points, it will be extremely difficult for them to derive any useful insights from them.

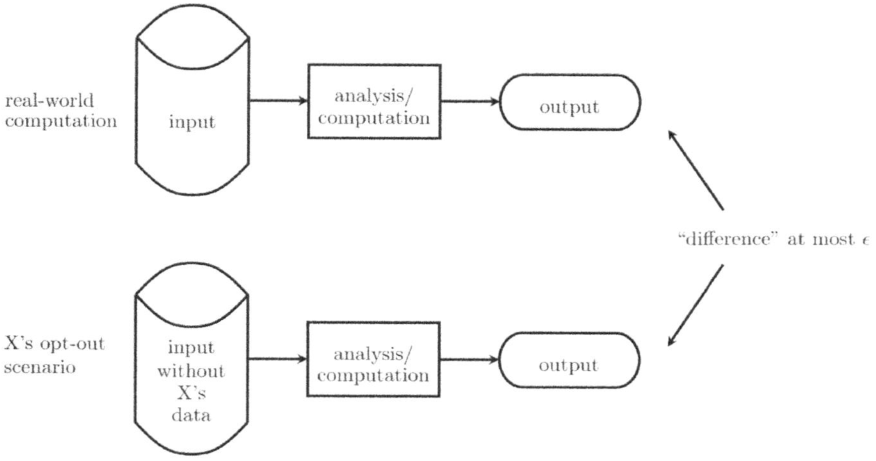

Figure 7: Differential Privacy

New developments in this area are investigating creative approaches to maximise the trade-off between privacy and utility. In order to maximise privacy protection while minimising the impact on data quality, researchers are inventing more effective noise infusion techniques. Furthermore, the incorporation of differential privacy into decentralised systems, such as federated learning setups, presents a promising strategy where data stays on individual devices and only aggregated insights are shared, minimising the centralization of sensitive data.

Future Directions and Possibilities

A wide range of new directions and opportunities are now possible because to the impressive developments that are expected in the fields of AI, machine learning, and network security. The creation of more complex and specialised models is one major direction in the fields of AI and machine learning. These models will not only perform better when it comes to translating languages, identifying images, and analysing data, but they will also show a greater comprehension of context and nuance. In order to make sure that AI systems are impartial, transparent, and accountable while also protecting privacy and human values, the development of AI ethics and responsible AI will become more prominent.

Additionally, there is a lot of potential in the merging of AI and other cutting-edge technologies, including quantum computing. Processing power will exponentially increase thanks to quantum AI, opening up hitherto unthinkable possibilities for solving complicated problems. Breakthroughs in areas including drug development, climate modelling, and optimisation problems may result from this combination.

The increasingly sophisticated cyber-attacks in the field of network security demand equally creative defence techniques. It is projected that AI-driven security systems would become more autonomous, quickly recognising, and countering assaults and weaknesses in real time. As attack patterns change, machine learning algorithms will adjust and learn from them, strengthening preventative defence measures. Furthermore, AI-powered threat hunting will probably become a key component of cybersecurity operations, allowing professionals to foresee and mitigate risks even before they manifest.

The idea of "zero-trust" security frameworks will spread, revolutionising conventional perimeter-based strategies. These frameworks rely on AI to continuously evaluate user and device behaviour, making sure that only authorised entities, regardless of their location, are permitted access. Securing connected devices will become more and more important as the Internet of Things (IoT) ecosystem expands. AI-driven anomaly detection will become essential for preventing breaches related to the Internet of Things.

As a preventative step, ethical hacking, which uses AI to simulate intrusions and reveal weaknesses, will become more commonly used. The window of exposure to potential risks will be smaller as a result of proactive repair being made easier. This strategy will however also call for a balance between security testing and potential abuse, highlighting the importance of moral AI use.

Conclusion

Privacy-enhancing AI technologies have the potential to fundamentally alter how we think about data privacy in the AI era. A good balance between innovation and personal privacy is becoming closer to reality as new developments continue to take place. We can usher in a time when AI and data privacy coexist by embracing these technologies.

Table 6: Summary of Future Directions for Privacy-enhancing AI Technologies

Future Direction	Description
Homomorphic Federated Learning	Combination of homomorphic encryption and federated learning for heightened security and privacy.
Blockchain-backed Privacy	Integration of AI and blockchain to enhance transparency, accountability, and data privacy.
AI-driven Privacy Policy Gen.	AI-assisted automation of privacy policy creation for accurate reflection of data usage, fostering user trust.

Made in the USA
Monee, IL
04 November 2026

67381305R00125